OUT OF PRACTICE

Rob Buckman is a regular contributor to Radio 4's *Start the Week* and was medical presenter for the TV science programme *Don't Ask Me*. He has a fortnightly column in *GP* and has written for a number of other magazines including *Punch*.

Together with fellow medic Chris Beetles, Rob Buckman wrote and performed a two-man stage revue at the Mermaid Theatre in London. They have recently appeared again together in their own TV comedy series *The Pink Medicine Show*.

Amazingly, Dr Buckman continues to practise as a registrar in a London teaching hospital. He is married (to a doctor) and has a young daughter. *Out of Practice* is his first book.

ROB BUCKMAN

OUT OF PRACTICE

illustrated by Bill Tidy

PAN BOOKS
LONDON AND SYDNEY

*Some of the items in this book first appeared
in Rob Buckman's regular column 'Out of Practice'
for GP magazine. 'Accident' and 'Language' originally
appeared in Punch under different titles.*

First published 1978 by Whizzard Press
in association with Andre Deutsch Ltd
This edition published 1980 by Pan Books Ltd,
Cavaye Place, London SW10 9PG
© Robert Buckman 1978
ISBN 0 330 26041 3
Set, printed and bound in Great Britain by
Cox & Wyman Ltd, Reading

to
two very great men:
Barry Amiel & Chris Frears

CONTENTS

ACCIDENTS

I've always been attracted by the world of theatre and bright lights so when I was old enough to go to drama school, my parents sent me to medical school. My love of the dramatic drew me towards the study of emergency medicine and I lived in hope of one day coming across a Spot so that I could be The Man On It. In fact nothing in the way of an emergency came in my direction until seven o'clock on a summer morning when I was riding on my motorbike to our hospital, St Nissen's. A woman on a moped in front of me got knocked over by a car. Now you would expect that to be like a play on the radio with a sort of scree-urrhh-crunch-tinkle-tinkle effect. It was nothing of the kind. It was more like a sort of whoops-a-flopsie, and there we were. A Spot.

I parked my bike and ran over to her; my lecture notes on emergency medicine flashed up in front of my eyes: 'Do not move patient . . . check for arterial haemorrhage . . . establish airway . . . cardiac output'; and, as I ran, I rehearsed my opening line: 'I am a doctor. Do not move this patient.' Unfortunately there was nobody trying to move her and I was therefore unable to make a big show of not moving her. This threw me for a moment, so I checked for arterial haemorrhage. There wasn't any.

I could see she had a compound fracture of the left tibia and fibula, a situation known in the traumatology racket as the Broken Leg Situation (BLS). But I wasn't going to jump to any slapdash conclusions and assume it was just a simple

BLS. Oh no, I was going to do it all by the book, or rather by my lecture notes, wasn't I? So I very politely wished her good morning and asked her if she had pain anywhere else, and in particular did it hurt to breathe in? She answered – equally politely – that no, it was only the leg that was hurting but that seemed to be quite enough to be getting on with. This proved to me that she was conscious and capable of making air come out of her lungs, which took us as far as paragraph three of my lecture notes.

I then knelt down and checked her skull for fractures, counted her arms and examined the shoulders for dislocation. This took care of paragraphs four, five and seven, so I went back to paragraph six: the flail chest.

Flail chest is a condition caused by multiple rib fractures in which a section of thoracic cage compresses and contuses lung tissue ... Well, I won't burden you with the technical details, but if you're in the traumatology racket, it's like an American aircraft carrier to a Kamikaze pilot, miss it and you're out of business. So I unzipped her windcheater and pressed on her sternum – forgetting to mention that I was a doctor. This was a most unfortunate omission, since I was dressed at the time in jeans and a silly T-shirt printed with JESUS SAVES – GREEN SHIELD STAMPS (which was thought to be pretty funny in my college days). Anyway, there I was in my casual attire, fumbling inside this lady's windcheater when the police arrived. I stopped what I was doing and looked up at them, and they looked down at me. I seemed to have two choices. I could either say: 'Good morning, I am a doctor and (having not moved the patient and checked for arterial haemorrhage) I was examining for flail chest.' Or I could run. There was nothing in my lecture notes to help me. One of the policemen took out his notebook. I put on my gravest bedside expression, took a deep breath – and ran.

The next time was in Hove. There was already a knot of passers-by gathered around the supine figure when I arrived,

and one man in a tweed jacket, tweed hat and (astonishingly) a tweed-covered pipe was kneeling by the victim's side. I brushed him aside and went into my 'haemorrhage-airway-cardiac-output' routine. Unfortunately, he refused to stay brushed aside, but leapt back shouting that he was a fully qualified instructor in First Aid with the St John Ambulance Brigade.

I was just going to reply that I was a real doctor, as it happens, and he was not to move this patient etc., etc., when we were both brushed aside by a lad of about eighteen. This newcomer didn't even look up as he went into the haemorrhage-airway-cardiac-output business, but muttered over his shoulder to Mr Tweed and me that we weren't to worry, he was a second-year medical student. He'd been at it for about seven seconds, while Tweed and I were thinking what to say next, when a lovely blonde lady rushed up to the scene and put her head to the victim's chest (the victim, all this while, being perfectly conscious and rather enjoying the attention). Aware of the tension in the air, the blonde lady looked up with a glance of modest pride and announced in a tone of complacent rapture, 'I am a social worker.'

I seemed to have two choices. For a moment I considered rushing round to the back of this knot of doctors *manqués* and then bursting through yelling, 'My auntie is a physiotherapist!' or maybe, 'My grandmother has shares in a firm that makes stethoscopes!' But eventually I took the second course and with the practised ease of a fully trained traumatologist, ran away.

Now I wouldn't like you to think that I never got my chance to render assistance to a haemorrhaging casualty. I got my chance alright a year later. Unfortunately, the casualty was me. I was the front-seat passenger when my friend Beetles drove his Mini – for reasons best known to himself – into the back of a lady's car at thirty miles an hour. The clasp on the seat belt had broken (honest!) and the first thing I knew about it was when I found myself looking at something like a force nine snow blizzard as I flew through the windscreen. I could hear Beetles about three feet behind me shouting, 'Sorry, Rob,' and I remember thinking how polite of him to apologize.

When the world stopped moving, I found that my face was covered with blood. Again my lecture notes flashed before my eyes and I suddenly thought of a page in *Gray's Anatomy*. I saw an illustration of a skull with all the arteries drawn in red. One of them emerges from a little hole in the eyebrow ridge and is called the supra-orbital artery. For some strange reason I got it into my head that this was the source of my bleeding. So I jammed my left index finger firmly to my left eyebrow ridge and leapt out of the car, yelling to Beetles in my best Kenneth More voice to get an ambulance because I'd pranged an artery.

A few interested passers-by had assembled to await developments and soon clustered around me, trying to make me lie down. But I was not to be outdone this time and announced in a very loud, clear voice, 'I am a doctor. Do not panic. Please assist any others who have been injured in this accident.' The passers-by said there weren't any others injured in this accident and why didn't I lie down. I ignored them and staggered around with my finger in my left eye but soon noticed that the bleeding didn't seem to be stopping.

It was then that I remembered that I had something much more prominent than my supra-orbital artery from which I could be bleeding, i.e. my nose.

My nose was bleeding, and I had my finger in my eye. Oh dear, how I wished I hadn't told all those people I was a doctor. Anyway, I clamped off my nose with my right hand but still didn't dare let go of my left eye. So with three of my seven facial orifices blocked up, I allowed myself to be led into a small hospital ten yards away. It turned out to be a community ante-natal clinic. They were very nice to me, although I was obviously haemorrhaging from the wrong end as far as they were concerned. They cleaned my face and then dressed the cuts with some very large, familiar-looking gauze pads. They explained, rather cautiously, that these particular gauze pads were not usually used for that purpose. I replied that, as a critical comment on my behaviour, they were quite apt. Beetles agreed.

AMBITION

Most doctors have the same ambition. They work twenty-four hours a day, seven days a week, healing the sick and alleviating misery so that one day they will become Foreign Secretary.

APPENDIX, THE

See the *Appendix*

BEGINNER'S LUCK

See *Venepuncture* (unless under eighteen).

BODYBUILDING

You may not know it, but the sport of bodybuilding is gathering a vast following in the United States and is about to invade Britain. I thought I'd better let you know. The figurehead of the invasion is called Arnold Schwarzenegger and the film in which he stars (from the book of the same name, based on the film) is called *Pumping Iron*. The title refers to the unnatural process of distending the muscle bulk with blood, and we doctors are now on the alert for ill-advised acolytes of this cult flooding into surgeries and casualty. (So far I haven't seen any, but we all remember the early days of the platform-heel shoe, and the hoola-hoop, and the Black Death.)

Speaking personally, when I was younger, even before I decided to be a doctor, I was struck by the glamour and the dazzle of the physique competitions and I was the only boy in my class who wanted to be Miss World. Of course, Fate willed otherwise and I was disqualified at a very early stage when it was found out that I had four 'O' levels.

Given this burning interest in physical culture, you may be asking, how is it that my body remains the puny sack of

gristle and giblets and monosodium glutamate that it is today. Well, the answer is that despite my ambition to sport biceps like a subcutaneous melon, I remained a cringing coward and never did Sports at school. Sports was something for which I brought a note to be excused from. (Note grammar.) (All the 'excused sports' boys were kept in to do extra English, you see.) In fact I brought an 'excused sports' note so regularly that after two years my parents went half-crazy trying to think up new excuses. As far as I know, I was the only boy in 3B to be excused games because of senile dementia. It may have lost me my chance at the Inter-House Shield, but it won my dad the Carnegie Prize for contemporary fiction.

I did badly at Gym, too. I remember one particularly gruelling work-out on the parallel bar (I couldn't manage both of them). I strained so hard, I almost ruptured my teeth. When I regained consciousness I asked the gym master about the possibilities of bodybuilding. He looked at my body and said that it didn't need building as much as demolition and planning permission for an office, and he tried to interest me in euthanasia.

Thus thwarted as an Adonis, I decided to be a genius. My careers master pointed out that other boys in my class had got their names down earlier (Hockney D., Frost D., and Gabor Z. Z.) (it was that sort of school). I took stock of this situation – I was an 84 pound weakling, an 84 IQ twitling and an 84 handicap golfer. I decided to be a doctor, in the hope of spending my life in an outpatient clinic and finding someone with a body weedier and more pathetic than mine.

So it was with great interest that I heard about 'Pumping Iron' from a frail ninety-year-old lady on the ward. Because of her extreme weakness and fragility, I had adopted the habit of visiting her early every morning for a bout of Indian wrestling. After I'd lost for the third week running, she told me about 'Pumping Iron'. It was a revelation.

At first I found the regime of exercises somewhat arduous,

but then I applied the true scientific approach as used by doctors all over the world when faced by something they can't cope with. I split 'Pumping Iron' into two easy stages – pumping and ironing. The ironing presented no problem once I'd got Johnny Weissmuller to help me tie on my apron. But the pumping proved to be too much, and after a fortnight, I got the garage attendant to do it for me. He was so good at it that, after a month, I let him do the ironing as well.

As a result, after only six months of the regime, I have developed a set of bulging, rippling, pulsating muscles all over my garage attendant, and I shall be entering him for the Mr Sump Oil award this year. Next year I'm putting him in for Mr Universe and probably the Ascot Gold Cup as well. And let's see any skinny weakling try to kick sand in his face then. Even if you could find any sand, you'd be thrown out of the Royal Enclosure.

Well there you are, an advance warning of the impending cult. Followers of the sport say that they are in effect pushing the human body and mind to its very limit. As a trained scientist I understand the processes underlying the limitations of mind and body only too well, and as a doctor I sometimes feel that I represent the lower limits of both.

BRAIN

The human brain is the greatest achievement in Nature, and is the result of centuries of evolution, months of careful planning and weeks of testing in the laboratory and on the road (see *Accidents*).

It might interest you to know that the idea of centralization of nerve tissue (i.e. one brain per animal) is relatively new. For instance, dinosaurs had two brains (sort of), one at the head end and the other at the tail end. This meant that, in an emergency, a dinosaur couldn't tell the difference between migraine and haemorrhoids. And we all know someone like that, don't we?

Anyway when the primeval swamps dried up the dinosaurs were forced to adapt and evolve. In fact they evolved into two groups of animals. One group kept the brain up at the head end, their tails got smaller, they developed lungs, warm-bloodedness, haircuts and finally the three-piece suit, and they became *Homo sapiens*. The other group of dinosaurs kept the brain at the tail end, lost the brain at the head end, adopted a crouching posture and thick scaly skin and became Estate Agents. As you know, Estate Agents never seem to worry at all about most of the things that would cause you or me no end of headaches, which therefore proves that their head-end brain has atrophied – like the appendix (but less likely to cause trouble). We may confidently await the forces of evolution wiping out the remnants of the Estate Agents by the week after next.

CHROMOSOMES

Q: How is it that just one set of human chromosomes is able to hold all the information to make up a complete human being?

A: Because they don't waste time watching television.

CLOTHES

When I was a medical student I wanted to be a surgeon, mainly because I have a very long nose and wide mouth but rather lovely eyes, so that when gowned and masked in theatre I can display my finer features and keep the coarser ones under wraps. In all honesty this is not a very good reason for wanting to be a surgeon, as the Professor of Surgery pointed out to me when I applied for a job with him. But in fact there were deeper motives behind my surgical aspirations – there were the green pyjamas.

You see surgeons spend most of their working day in theatre and for every session they put on a clean pair of 'theatre greens'. These consist of a short-sleeved top which is so baggy round the shoulders that everyone can see your armpits and a pair of trousers that were apparently designed to fit a grand piano. Yet, however ill fitting, those green pyjamas solved the two greatest problems that I've always had with clothes – choosing them and ironing them.

I'm no good with clothes. As regards my wit, my friends have compared me to Oscar Wilde or Noel Coward, but for clothes I'm a Patrick Moore or a Gertrude Shilling. The main problem is that when I go out to buy clothes I lose my cool completely and become a babbling moron. You may not believe this but I once bought a pair of trousers with silver buttons up the side. I remember thinking as I tried them on, these are absurd, but the shop assistant told me that the manager's brother wore them. I bet he did, and I bet he looked just as much a berk as I did in them. The worst thing about these trousers was that the silver buttons really did up, or rather undid. When I took them out for a test drive at a party in Hampstead, some joker undid the buttons while I was chatting up a blonde secretary from a jam-packing plant. Without realizing it, I was walking around with my trousers slashed open up to the mid-thigh like a sort of male Suzie Wong. Only instead of looking sleek like Ms Wong (which wasn't the effect I was after anyway), I looked ragged, like Jungle Jim after being chased by the Zulus for an hour. I may not see that manager's brother again, but if I do, he'll be easy enough to recognize.

Since that pair, every other pair of trousers I've had has gone baggy at the knees – sometimes even before I've got them out of the paper bag. In fact clothes behave so badly with me that even my gloves are beginning to go baggy at the knees.

But, however gross, my gullibility isn't my only millstone in the clothes shops; I also have this lethal tendency to snap up anything reduced for clearance. That habit started with a pair of suede Chelsea boots reduced from five pounds to three (this was in 1969, you know). Unfortunately they were also reduced from size ten to size eight. My sense of economy and fashion overcame everything except, eventually, the pain which brought tears to my eyes. I felt like an eighteenth-century lady in a whalebone corset – in fact it was the general opinion of my associates that my feet actually look better in a whalebone corset, and my head in a bustle. I ignored the ribaldry but sadly failed to learn the lesson that (in the words of an old joke) when you buy a car dirt-cheap, you realize how hard it is to drive a bargain.

But even when I'm not wearing pantomime trousers and winkle-pickers I look absurd and scruffy. I can't help it. Even in my best suit (interviews/funerals/bar mitzvahs) I look like a beanbag that's just been demobbed. Of course when I try to look casual, I do look relaxed. Everyone agrees on that. I do look *very* relaxed as if, they say, I'd been sleeping in my clothes, in a hedge possibly, for a week at least.

Which is why I wanted to be a surgeon. It's not that green suits me; it's just that it doesn't suit anybody else either. And in the green pyjamas *everybody's* arms look scrawny and pathetic, and you can see up everybody's armpits. I was extremely happy poncing about in my democratic non-discriminating theatre greens, and it was only when I realized that surgeons work an average 100 hour week that I decided to find some other solution to my lack of dress sense.

Having decided to be a physician, I then had to make a big decision: hospital medicine, or general practice? Once again, I delved deep into my soul. General practice offered a gentler lifestyle, closer involvement with the community and the opportunity for long-term care, whereas the false, shallow, back-stabbing cut-throat world of hospital medicine offered long white coats; long white coats which could be buttoned down to the knee and up to the mid-chest. This would mean that I need only display (and iron) the collar of my shirt and the bottom six inches of my trousers; in fact if I could learn a good Scottish accent and stick a dagger into my socktops, I might get away without trousers altogether.

The rest is history. I'm now a hospital registrar and wear the standard St Nissen's registrar's outfit – striped shirt (collar) and corduroy trousers (cuffs). Even so, I've had little peace. One nurse said I always looked as if I had to be back in Millett's window by midnight. I found that discouraging and considered going round in hospital plastic refuse bags. These bags are tough and durable, commodious and modest, and available in a wide range of colours. That was the problem, I couldn't choose between pink (for swill), blue (for foul linen) or a rather fetching grey (for typhoid or hepatitis).

Well, that's the situation in a nutshell. All I can suggest to anybody who may have a similar worry is, come and be a hospital registrar – the manager's brother is one.

DESCARTES

Descartes is probably best remembered for his famous saying *cogito ergo sum* (I think, therefore I am). However, as far as we humble doctors are concerned, his most valuable contribution was what he said about the human mind. Basically, he suggested that the mind lived inside the body and worked it like a signalman in his box at a railway junction. Now that may sound a pretty silly idea since it immediately poses the question, 'Who gives the signalman his orders?' In other words, what makes the human mind work in the first place? But in fact Descartes' notion was quite a good one for the time, since it allowed seventeenth-century scientists to study the human body in isolation, as it were. They could look at, say, an arm and study it like a bit of machinery, instead of having to worry about mystical forces and causes supposedly lodged inside it. The problems of this 'ghost-in-machine' idea only came three hundred years later, but we're working on them right now. Honest.

I only give you this information because I toyed with the idea of writing a biography of Descartes for a long time (about eight minutes in all). I thought that you might be interested in the material that I gathered for it, though I could be wrong. Anyway, here is the masterpiece so far:

'The main theme of Descartes' life and destiny can be determined simply by examining his name. In the seventeenth century his name was spelt "Rene Des Cartes". Translated into English this becomes "Irene of the Maps" or maybe "Irene of the Menus". It is therefore clear that Descartes was destined, from the start, to become a woman fond of travelling and eating. Had restaurants been invented in time, he would have been a female Egon Ronay. In the event, they weren't, so he wasn't.

'In his early notebooks it is possible to see those two major themes emerge and crystallize. Much of what is written in those early works has never been revealed to the public or even to me, and I am thus reduced to conjecture and hypothesis. By the age of eighteen, Descartes had already written: "I travel, therefore I eat"; and by twenty-one he had experimented with: "I eat, therefore I travel" and "I am eating, therefore I must be travelling." After an unsuccessful attempt at naïve Primitivism ("I travel in order to eat"), he arrived at his final formulation: "I have just eaten, therefore I must now travel"; in one fell swoop anticipating the development of the railway buffet car and Enterovioform.

'Contemporary records suggest that in 1617 he travelled from France to Holland. In 1619, he travelled to (and ate in) Bavaria. Returning to Holland in 1629 he was just in time to catch the 1649 to Sweden, changing carriages in Luxembourg in 1630 and changing socks in Liechtenstein in 1641. And not a moment too soon. During all that time, not only was he travelling and eating, but, brilliant philosopher that he was, he was thinking as well. And it was probably in the ten years that he spent on the station platform in Holland that he came up with the *cogito ergo sum* dictum that rocketed him to the top of the charts (or des Cartes, as they're known in French).

'Having taken the first steps along the road to materialist dualism, Descartes stopped thinking and therefore died. It is of historical curiosity (and limited news value) to note that after his death his career as a traveller continued unabated. Buried in Sweden in 1650, his body was removed to Paris in 1666 to get a better view of the Fire of London. In 1819 it was removed once again, this time to St Germain dis Pris

28

(translation: St Germain, second prize), where I am told it currently awaits refreighting to an out-of-town try-out in Hove. If that is successful, we may expect to see the Descartes corpse as a one-man travelling show arriving in London's West End next year, provisionally entitled *No Sex Please, We Think We're Dead*.

'As Abraham Petersdorf has said, "The man who thought and was, is dead and well, and certain that he has been." How many of us can say the same?'

Well, that's as far as I got with my biography. Not bad for a whole afternoon, eh?

DOCTORS – (A BISHOP SPEAKS)

The medical profession throughout the centuries has always been held in the highest regard by the medical profession. However there once was a Bishop of Salisbury called John Earle (born 1601) who defined a physician as follows:

'He is indeed only languaged in diseases and speaks Greek many times when he knows not [see *Jargon*]. If he have been but a by-stander at some desperate recovery, he is slandered with it though he be guiltless [see *Beginner's Luck*]. If you send this [urine] to him you must resolve to be sick howsoever, for he will never leave examining your water till he has shaked it into a disease. If he sees you himself his presence is the worst visitation: for if he cannot heal your sickness, he will be sure to help it. In conclusion he is a sucking consumption, and very brother to the worms, for they are ingendered out of man's corruptions' [see *Dogs*].

The Salisbury Area Health Authority have told me that for some unaccountable reason, after 300 years or more, John Earle is still very low on the waiting list for his hernia operation. Tee hee hee.

DOGS

The question is often asked: is the National Health Service going to the dogs? Speaking personally, I think a much more important question is: will the dogs still be there when we arrive? My own prediction is that they won't. By 1988 I think the dogs will have left, and by 1992 we shall meet them coming the other way. I was once asked to speak in a debate entitled 'The National Health Service – Whither?' and I said, 'Yes, it might.'

ECGs

ECG stands for Electrocardiogram and is a record of the electrical activity of the heart. It is recorded (painlessly and under no obligation to the customer) as a series of squiggles on paper that looks like ticker tape. Interpreting the ECG requires a great deal of skill and is rather similar to (although less difficult than) reading the small print on insurance policies. (see *X, Doctor*)

EMERGENCY! WARD ... UMM ...

Every hospital has its Apocrypha, a fund of stories of highly dubious origin attributed by different generations to a selection of past luminaries. My own teaching hospital, St Nissen's, has a wonderful old chestnut concerning a physician (now deceased) of such eminence that the mere mention of his name was said to cure scrofula, banish warts and crack mirrors at fifty yards. However before his rise to greatness he, like ordinary mortals, had to serve his six months as a house surgeon. His boss was a highly revered general surgeon and, at the time of the story (anywhere between 1904 and 1931), the reputation of St Nissen's seemed to rest on this one surgical genius. As a result, he was treated with the distant respect and obeisance worthy of a cross between God and Red Rum.

Anyway his reverence, the Notable Surgeon, was engaged in some bowel surgery or other with our eminence-in-embryo, his houseman, attached to the other end of a retractor keeping the patient's liver out of his boss's field of action. After they'd been at it an hour or so, the Notable Surgeon realized that the patient's arteries suddenly weren't pulsating the way they ought to be, and mentioned this to the anaesthetist. The anaesthetist immediately – and correctly – diagnosed cardiac arrest, that is, the sudden cessation of the heart's action.

Nowadays, we have a system of emergency calls which brings the cardiac arrest team to the theatre in less than three minutes, but in those days everyone just had to shift for themselves. The Notable Surgeon was very cool and simply took a scalpel, went up through the diaphragm and began massaging the patient's heart from inside the chest. His houseman in the meantime – even at that stage of his career thinking like a true physician – rushed into the anteroom and grabbed the emergency drugs box. This contained a syringe of adrenalin which in these circumstances can restart the heart. He fitted the syringe with the long flexible needle specially designed to inject the drug straight into the heart, and rushed back into the theatre. Here, he swiftly plunged the needle in between the patient's fifth and sixth ribs, through the skin and straight into the Notable Surgeon's hand.

Astonishingly, for this was the era before antibiotics, the Notable Surgeon survived. Even more astonishingly, so did his houseman. Several of his colleagues and members of the nursing staff suggested that he do the honourable thing, that is, commit suicide. (Or maybe the honourable thing was to marry one of the nurses. I forget.) Anyway, he did neither, but rose to fame; and his story is told to every junior who feels that he's just committed the blunder to end all blunders. I've been told it dozens of times.

I don't know what it is, but there is something about those

emergencies, that cry of 'crash-call', that turns perfectly self-respecting juniors into hare-brained Errol Flynns, leaping around and buckling swashes as if there was no tomorrow.

It's happened to me often enough. The 'crash-call' system at St Nissen's was a model of efficient simplicity. Anyone dialling the crash-call number rings a very *very* loud red telephone in the casualty department. This is answered by the nearest staff nurse, while the casualty officer, plus another nurse and a porter, run to the door of the casualty department (ten yards from the phone and on the way to the main hospital). The nurse who answers the phone finds out which ward the call is coming from and shouts it to the team who then run there, picking up an emergency trolley on the way. On my first day as casualty officer, I was all set. I'd got myself some smart shoes with special metal heel crescents so that I could make a lot of noise in the corridors and clear everyone out of my way. Oh yes, I was ready all right. The first crash-call came at noon. I heard the very loud telephone, ran to the door of the department, and I was off.

I noted with some satisfaction that I was down the stairs and into the underground corridor ahead of the rest of the team, and my shoes were making a very impressive CLACKCLACKIT-CLACKCLACKIT. Full of urgent self-importance, I ran past a friend of mine and shouted 'Crash-call!' as I shot by. 'Where?' he called after me. I skidded to a halt.

I suddenly realized that I didn't know which ward I was meant to be going to. I'd run off without waiting to listen to the nurse who answered the phone. No wonder I was ahead of everyone else. Since the hospital had thirty-two wards scattered over three blocks, to run to each one and ask if they'd put out the crash-call would have taken me roughly four days. I had no choice but to run back to the casualty department. I felt very silly as I ran back, and tried to make my shoes sound less noisy (which they wouldn't). I sneaked back into the department, hoping desperately that no one had seen my idiotic sprint. I tried to control my breathing and sauntered into sister's office.

'I thought I heard the crash-call bell a few minutes ago.'

'Yes,' sister said, 'it was a wrong number.'

'Oh right. Fine, fine, fine,' I said as casually as I could, considering my breathlessness, and turned to go.

'Oh, Dr Buckman,' sister said, 'next time don't start running till you find out where to go.'

Astonishingly, I survived.

After six months in the department, like most of the crash-call team, I got totally conditioned by that phone. When I was on night duty, I used to sleep on a trolley in a cubicle next to it so that I would be first off the mark, and I got so attuned that I would leap up at the first loud TINK that it gave before ringing properly. This had unfortunate side-effects for me after I moved on from casualty. I once fell asleep in a barber's chair while my hair was being washed. (Actually I'd only gone into the shop to look at the pornographic magazines, but after two hours, they insisted that I have a haircut. That's why I fell asleep.) Anyway my head was right next to the telephone, which suddenly rang. In true Pavlovian style, I leapt up, ran to the door of the shop and shouted: 'WHERE IS IT?' The barber thought I was a jewel thief on the run. In fact, he still does. To be honest, I prefer the *frisson* of being mistaken for an international criminal to the endless questions about impotence and baldness I get asked when barbers find out I'm a doctor.

I suppose every job gives you moments when you feel that you're the biggest idiot to disgrace the earth, and that if there were such a thing as natural justice you'd be exterminated in a bolt of lightning. I've felt like that hundreds of times and that story from our Apocrypha has always been enormous consolation to me. At least, I say to myself, I've never stabbed the Professor of Surgery in the hand. But only because he wouldn't keep still long enough.

FACE

Medically speaking, the face is very important. As a doctor, I spend all day looking out of mine and into other people's and to be quite frank I'd be lost without it. You see, from the evolutionary point of view, the survival value of the human face was enormous, in that during mankind's evolution it became possible to distinguish – by the face – the front of the head from the back. This was important because the eyes are in the front of the head, and if you had no way of telling front from back, you might find yourself walking backwards and not see where you were going. This would have been a grave disadvantage in the Pleistocene era and also in central Birmingham before the advent of the pedestrian precinct.

But it was during the Victorian epoch that the face came under closest scrutiny, especially before breakfast. The Victorians had a great mania for classifying things. They felt that if you could subdivide everything there was in the whole world, you could understand it. In many ways this was their basic ideal of science; and when they applied it to the study of the face, they called it Physiognomy.

Now you might think that it would be a complete waste of time but according to the *Encyclopaedia of Face and Form Reading or Personal Traits Both Physical and Mental Revealed by Outward Signs Through Practical and Scientific Physiognomy* (Mary Olmsted Stanton, 1895) the study of physiognomy is essential to 'actors, lawyers, bankers, superintendents of asylums, the unmarried, and railroad managers'. Not having met a railroad manager who was well versed in physiognomy (or indeed anything), I eagerly looked up the section on the railways and there found that 'if you are about employing a man for a certain line of duty in the railroad service and he has some very peculiar gestures, [this book will tell you] what signification if any they have in revealing his character or capabilities'. Not having the advantage of an education in physiognomy, I have nevertheless had no difficulty in understanding the peculiar gestures of railroad employees; indeed one railroad employee of my acquaintance has a set of Peculiar Gestures so virulent that he picks up extra money on Sundays by bleaching calico with them at a distance of ten yards.

Anyway the basis of physiognomy is the subdivision of the face into the various features: nose, chin, lips, eyes (Get the idea? Tell me if I'm going too fast for you.), and the classification of those features into types. Here, as an example, are the kinds of nose you can have: 'snub type, *retroussé* type, embryotic, infantoid, idiotic, literary type, critic's type, commercial type, dishonest type, with or without Revengeful Nostrils, and abnormal type'. You will notice that a critic's nose is not a literary one, a truth I have suspected for many years. You will also be alarmed to hear that the distinction between the commercial nose and the dishonest one is very slight and cannot be detected without seven years study either of Physiognomy or Accountancy.

I'm afraid that the *Encyclopaedia* is not very specific about the 'abnormal' type of nose, apart from saying that it occurs on aboriginal women's faces. I would have thought an aboriginal woman's nose *could* be considered abnormal if it occurred on the face of, say, the Duke of Marlborough (even more abnormal if it occurred on his chest) but why every aboriginal woman should be considered abnormal simply by the shape of her nose, I cannot say. Perhaps I should be asking an aboriginal man.

I was surprised that, despite the great variety of eyes, lips and cheeks, there are only three types of centre-of-chin. As you can see from the accompanying illustration from the *Encyclopaedia*, if the centre of your chin is flat or stupid,

FIG. 138.—Flat, or Stupid.   FIG. 139.—Convex, or Brutal.   FIG. 140.—Indented.
(A SIMPLETON.)   (A MALEFACTOR.)   (EDWARD EVERETT.)

then you are a SIMPLETON, if it's convex or brutal you are a MALEFACTOR, if it's indented you're EDWARD EVERETT. And if you are indented and Edward Everett put the money in the usual place tonight and the other members of the choir need never know.

As demonstrations of the power and range of the study of physiognomy, Miss Stanton goes on to analyse portraits of leading figures. Look, for example, at the woodcut of John Ruskin ('Author, Art Critic'). What does the educated physi-

FIG. 66.—JOHN RUSKIN. (AUTHOR, ART CRITIC.)

ognomist see? Well for a start, the physiognomist does *not*
see what appears to be a perforated bogie dangling from the
art critic's left nostril but instead goes straight on to report
'the domestic faculties of this character are unevenly developed. Height of the point of the nose from the plane of
the face shows Human Nature; the droop of the septum,
Hope and Analysis; at the express tip we find Mental Imitation large; while in close contiguity are the signs for Ideality. Sublimity, Constructiveness, Acquisitiveness, Veneration,
Locality, Prescience, Order and Time. The hair in the
arrangement above the forehead shows inventive capacity.'
If Ruskin had brushed it the other way, it would have shown
his Hatred of Solicitors and his Inability to Fill in Forms
Properly. If he had brushed it straight back it would have
shown his Bald Patch.

Similarly the portrait of Joanna Southcott ('Founder of a
Religious Sect, Fanatic, Prophetess, and Imposter') shows 'in
the nose the signs for Human Nature, Ideality, Veneration

FIG. 87.—JOANNA SOUTHCOTT. (FOUNDER OF A
RELIGIOUS SECT, FANATIC, PROPHETESS, AND
IMPOSTOR.)

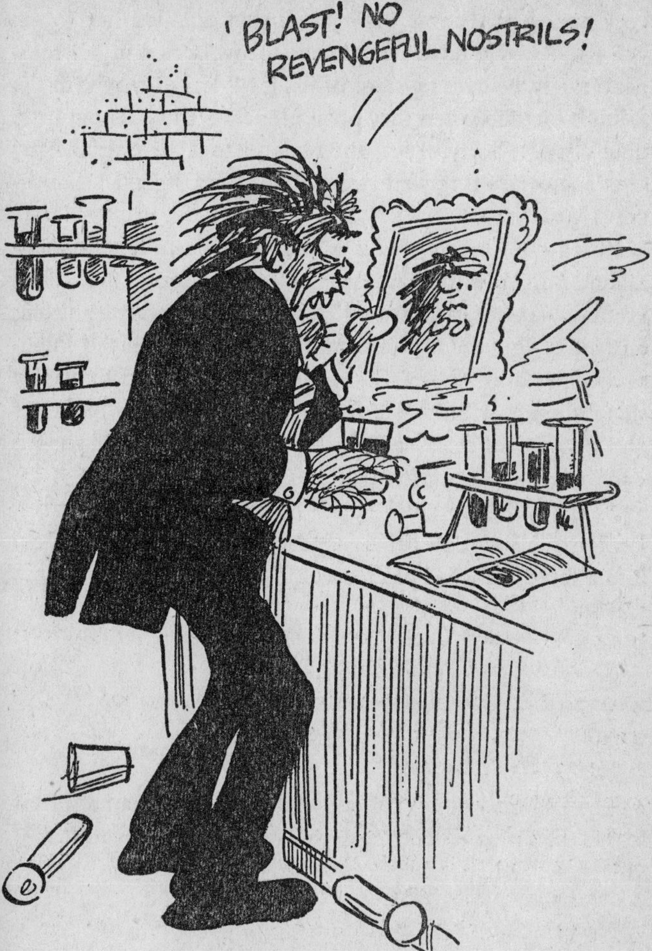
'BLAST! NO REVEVENGEFUL NOSTRILS!

and Self-Will. The region about the eyes is very peculiar. Form and Size are wonderfully developed. Credenciveness is very apparent. It was these traits that enabled her to see visions.' I would have thought the arrow buried in her forehead might be causing some of the trouble, but maybe in the fullness of time when they open Her Box, there'll be a little note saying: 'Sorry, it was the region about my eyes and my Credenciveness that were doing it all along, signed J. Southcott (Miss).'

I used the *Encyclopaedia* to look up my own face (though a hand mirror would have been better) and found that I lack Human Nature, Ideality and Veneration but am very strong on Not Paying the Gas Bill, and have well-developed Pneumativeness and Abusive Language. My nose and upper lip show abundant Strength, Stamina and Stoutness of Heart and also reveal that I am, in fact, a race horse and should win the 3.30 at Kempton Park if it comes up mud.

As the wrinkled old Chinese men say in the take-out in Pentonville Road on Friday nights: 'There is a lot that goes into a face, but what you get out of it depends on how close you stand.'

FAT

I once knew a woman patient who lost fifteen pounds of fat in less than a week. She left it on the bus and I found it.

FOOD (HOSPITAL CANTEEN)

Hospital food is a thing apart. It really is. St Nissen's canteen was, for a time, the only place in Britain where you could get a meat and four vegetables, of which three were potatoes.

The people who serve the stuff to the poor saps are almost always Spanish and Portuguese and the language barrier seems to protect them against appreciating the finer meanings of the expletives thrown at them by the students and staff. I remember one of my braver colleagues once taking a plate of chilli con carne back to the chef and asking him what it was. 'Eez cheely-con-carny ... cheely is means "beans", con is means "with" and carny is means "more beans".'

When I moved further north to the Witheringham hospital, the canteen was supervised by a massive Portuguese lady who only pronounced the first three letters of any word. This made ordering a meal a rather random procedure and we were all amazed when 'greafi' turned out to be grilled fish and 'roptay' came out as roast potatoes. However her favourite dessert was jelly and every single day of the year, next to the cheese-and-biscuits section, there stood a huge Pyrex dish filled full of a jelly of some lurid colour. Usually it was either bright yellow, deep orange or fluorescent green, but one day it was an extraordinarily deep and alarming vermilion. I asked her, 'What flavour is that then?' She looked at it, 'Eez ... red.' She was absolutely right.

GIFTS

Before I qualified I had the idea that patients were always rewarding their doctors with gifts. I suppose I'd watched too much Dr Finlay on the box, but I must say the concept was reinforced when I moved into my present house which had previously been a GP's home and surgery. On the first Christmas Eve the doorbell rang constantly, and I opened the door to a succession of middle-aged Cypriots clutching bottles wrapped in brown paper.

As it happens, I was never the kind of person patients wanted to give gifts to. I never had the necessary air of blithe charisma and super-cool. I think I was generally too nervous (see *Goofs*) and carried an air of well-meaning anxiety, which checked the unstinting generosity of my various customers. If they'd wanted to give me a gift, it would probably have been a bottle of valium or a fortnight on a health farm.

In fact, after a year in medicine, I was given a gift and I shall never forget it. I was looking after a seriously handicapped old lady and had invented a few little tricks and gizmoes to help her cope with the wheelchair and bell push. When she was ready to leave hospital, she called me over and gave me a bulky paper bag.

'It's not much,' she said, 'but it's the thought that counts.' After she'd left, I opened my present. It was four pairs of string underpants.

In the privacy of my home (with no obligation to me or the purchaser – I am over eighteen), I tried them on. If you

45

have never seen yourself in string underpants, let me recommend it to you as an exercise in ego-stripping. As I examined my reflection in the mirror, I thought it looked rather as if I was carrying my generative apparatus home in a shopping bag. When the old lady said it's the thought that counts, I wonder if it had been the thought of me wearing the underpants that had stimulated her. Knowing her sense of humour, I think it probably was. I wonder what Dr Cameron would have said. Or what he would have looked like in string underpants.

GOOFS

Every doctor makes mistakes occasionally, and there's an old proverb to the effect that any doctor who says he's never made a single mistake is either too stupid to realize that he isn't clever enough to spot his own stupidity, or else he's a bloody liar. If you study this book carefully (and now that you've paid for it, you might just as well) you'll find that it is peppered with examples of my own mistakes, goofs and minor idiocies. Mercifully none of them has produced any serious ill-effects for the patients concerned, but these moments of boob (or vice versa – see *Undressing*) have always caused a florid reaction in myself.

It's a very nasty sensation when you realize you've done something wrong. The first thing that happens to me is that I get a strange feeling of distance, as if the whole world was rushing away from me at great speed (sometimes of course it actually is – but I attribute that to my rather cheap and offensive after-shave lotion). The next thing that happens is that I get a damp crinkly feeling under my collar as if my neck were suddenly three sizes too small for its skin. This is accompanied by a prickly burning sensation at the tips of both ears and I can usually hear my blood singing through

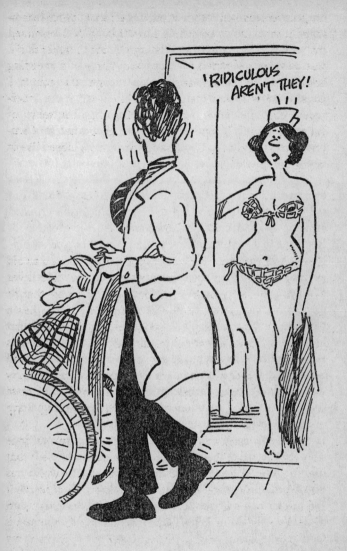

my ear lobes. This sensation is quickly replaced by a desire to grow a beard and get a job as a beach boy in Acapulco. In fact at one stage I was so terrified of making mistakes that I used to carry a Mexican Airlines flight schedule in my white coat. However I soon gave that idea up when I realized I couldn't grow a beard.

As I've got older and more experienced in the art of clinical medicine this 'panic reaction' hasn't got any less or any more rare; I've just got better at disguising it, like a schoolboy who folds his pocket hanky so that the snotty bits don't show. But the strangest aspect of it all is that these reactions bring with them a feeling of isolation – I always think I'm the only person in the world to be reduced to this crinkled cringing heap. I certainly never expected those of Senior Registrar or Consultant rank to be plagued by such symptoms. I was wrong.

I was attending a symposium at one of the Royal Colleges of Physicians last year. A symposium is really only a posh word for a conference or shindig and always has a rather carefree carnival air about it. Grey-haired distinguished luminaries from all over the world gather to listen to and talk at other grey-haired distinguished luminaries, while pin-striped junior sycophants try and get a word in edgeways. Anyway, after each lecture there is a period of mass showing off called question time. This gives the punters a chance to reveal their true genius. The usual trick is to take a fact of medicine so esoteric that no one present could possibly have heard of it and turn it into a question by prefacing it with: 'Would Professor Schmaltz agree that ...?' With a bit of luck Professor Schmaltz is completely stumped, and the punter can go back to his own hospital after the symposium as the Man Who Baffled Schmaltz of Edinburgh. You get the idea.

Now, before anyone says anything at a symposium he has to introduce himself. Traditionally this is done in the style of *University Challenge* with a brusque cry of 'Endlebaum,

Bristol' or 'Perkins, Sheffield' or whatever. (In fact the habit becomes so ingrained that I once saw a cardiologist catch his fingers in the revolving door at the college and shout, 'Jesus! Nazareth.') It was on one lazy summer afternoon in the post-prandial stupor that accompanies the first lecture after lunch that I was privileged to observe what I had previously assumed to be my own panic-reaction in a consultant.

One of the myriad shirt-sleeved boy wonders stood up at question time to divest himself of his intellectual nugget; only he got so excited he blew his cool. He began, 'Arnold, Durham ... no, sorry, I mean Birmingham. I don't know why I said Durham actually, I've never even been there.' Oh, it was lovely! Hansard might have said 'there was laughter'; in fact, there was mass leg wetting. Professors with half an alphabet after their name wept with laughter. Fat biochemists weak with hilarity had to rest their heads on wizened endocrinologists. Even a few of the neurologists laughed and up till then most of them were thought to have been dead.

And during all this the Poor Sap who started it all stood there and exhibited the panic reaction – his neck bristled, his ears tingled and he shuffled from foot to foot. Suddenly I realized I was not alone in idiocy. I was merely one of a large number of identical fallible parts in a huge fallible machine – a pawn in a vast incomprehensible pawn cocktail.

Actually while I was writing this section I came upon an even more exquisite example of the public goof which I hope you'll forgive me for mentioning. I went on a march to demonstrate against the National Front, organized by the Anti-Nazi League; and a superb affair it was, too. We were marching along the Strand in the middle of about 30,000 people when the bloke next to me suddenly shouted out as loudly as he could, 'NATIONAL FRONT!' We all turned to look at him, and, being British, nobody wanted to be the first to say, look, old chap, we're the Opposition. Anyway, a second later he threw back his head and shouted again,

'NATIONAL FRONT!' We all turned round once more, and he went very red in the face and said, 'Look here, when I shout "National Front!" you're all meant to shout "OUT!" and then I do it again and you all shout "OUT! OUT! OUT!"' And we all said, oh I *see*, yes, that makes sense, et cetera. In that moment we all realized that he was one of us, and indeed, that we were several of him.

I only tell the story to illustrate the point that no one is free from the occasional goof and that most of them, however bad they appear at the time, can be smoothed out eventually. Provided of course that you don't go round telling people that you've never been to Durham.

HANDSHAKE, THE

For many years I thought that 'condescension' was what made the mirror in the bathroom all foggy. Then I became a doctor, and learnt what it really meant. Take, for example, our attitude as doctors to the routine physical examination of our patients. As a student, I was once harangued for fifteen minutes by a consultant neurologist on the need to shake hands with the patient at the beginning of the interview. It was not merely the first step on the road to a properly based psycho-dynamic doctor-patient relationship, he said (no, no, no, we all said), but it was an important way of picking up valuable clues to the patient's physical illnesses (yes, yes, yes, we all nodded) and may be the first hint of over-active thyroid, an anxiety state or even a rare skin disease that makes the hands stiff and cadaverous, called scleroderma. Good Lord, we all thought, fancy forgetting a handshake and missing out on the rare diagnosis of scleroderma. How dreadful. Quick, lads, get in there, pump the old bunches of fives and root out all that wicked old scleroderma.

At lunch that day, I found out from a disloyal neurology registrar that they'd only seen one case of scleroderma in the last five years and that particular consultant had forgotten to shake hands, had missed the diagnosis and had been boring the arse off his students ever since. While we're on the subject, I would like to mention that, since then, I actually *did* diagnose a case of scleroderma at the first handshake, and, exultant with joy, opened the referral letter from the GP to find that he had diagnosed it first three months ago and would I please do something about the patient's gastric ulcer? My lesson from that incident was to forget the initial handshake and read the GP's letter.

So why do doctors shake hands with patients? Could it be to establish physical contact? Surely not. In a few minutes the doctor will be prying into his patient's innermost recesses with tubes and lights and gloves; and what could be more physical than that? (This is not a quiz. Humorous replies will be mercilessly plagiarized and no royalties paid.) Well then, do we shake hands in the hope of that rare diagnostic coup? Never. For a start since the important signs we are looking for are increased sweatiness of the patient's hand, or shaking or stiff skin, most of us can hardly tell whether our patient's hand is sweatier, shakier or stiffer than our own in the first place. Secondly, on the one occasion when it might give us the diagnosis we forget to shake hands anyway (see above).

Some authorities have suggested that the handshake is an expression of sympathy. But just think about it. What could be less sympathetic than a handshake? For a start, the doctor has no idea, at the outset, what is wrong with the patient, so his sympathy, however bountiful, is going to be pretty random. And later, when he does know what the trouble is, the last way to express sympathy is to shake hands. A hug, a double-cheek kiss or even an arm round the shoulder and a chuck under the chin might be reasonable, but a handshake doesn't convey an attitude, it merely records an event, like a parking ticket or a tombstone.

It is my belief that the handshake has grown up in the tradition of medicine, because it is usually unexpected and therefore *totally unnerves the patient*. It puts the patient into the feudal serf position, makes them feel patronised and insecure and, in the complex jargon of doctor-patient socio-dynamics, scares the pants off them. In addition, I think that most patients are already apprehensive about their visit to the doctor and many feel aggressive as a reflection of that insecurity. The handshake proves the doctor is totally secure. For a start it signifies, so the anthropologists say, that the doctor is not carrying an offensive weapon (or not in that hand, at that moment anyway). Thus the doctor is saying: Look, I'm so confident of victory that I can offer this submissive gesture even *au dehors de combat* (French for *avant la bataille*), and also, look, I haven't got thyrotoxicosis, warts or scleroderma.

There may be even more to it than that. The handshake in some way reduces the likelihood of the patient sueing the doctor later on. A perfect illustration of this came about when I saw an American (high-risk litigant) lady with abdominal pain in casualty. I took a careful history which received cursory and frigid replies, loaded with menace and future *subpoenae*. Undaunted, I began my examination and then asked her to breathe out while I smelled her breath for signs of ketosis or foetor (both of which might be clues to her problem). This is regarded as the most proper way to do things (I was a real ponce in those days). (I still am.) Anyway, she was horrified, but I persisted, wearing an air of clinical gravity, mixed with detached self-effacement and served with lashings of modest altruism and low-cholesterol schmaltz. She was totally disarmed and later even sent me a book token which I converted into a regular subscription to a current professional journal called *Playboy*.

Now, whenever I sense that I am being threatened by a patient I do everything to make them aware of my condescension. I shake their hand. I smell their breath. Probe their armpits. Flex their socks. Suck their shoelaces. Shine a torch through their toenails. And all with an air of seriousness and humility that makes them wish they'd never been born with an armpit, nostril or toe.

Well, there you are, a real trade secret. That's my view of

how the tradition of handshaking grew up. After all, as one consultant said many years ago, a consultation may only be a matter of life or death to the patient, but for the doctor it's his whole career. And if that doesn't get my hand shaking, nothing will.

HORMONES

Hormones are the chemicals responsible for all the biological luxuries of human existence, e.g. metabolism, growth, sex, colour television and matching airport luggage. A lecturer in my first year explained that 'whereas your nerves are like telephone lines carrying electrical information instantly, your hormones are like chemical postmen'. In my own case they were *exactly* like postmen; they dawdled on the way, lost several of the most important letters, went on strike for (apparently) seven years and then arrived early in the morning and woke me up by rattling my chemical letterbox. As a result puberty in my case was delayed until I was nearly twenty and had almost given up. After puberty (the following Saturday, in fact) I *did* give up.

Hormones, being indirectly responsible for the emotion of love are therefore the greatest single source of human misery since the invention of British Rail coffee. My researches in this field led me to what I now believe is the earliest record of the destructive effect of the androgenic steroids. It is called 'Y Lovelesse Kynge' ('The King Without Love') and it epitomizes the prose fragments of the fifteenth century in that it is totally incomprehensible:

Onnce inne a tymme before thatte many of us wir borne, they're livd, in a Castille Highe and Mightie, a Kynge Who Knew Notte Whatte Love was.

Nowe thenn, thisse Kynge hadde him a Daughterre nearlie the

mooste bewtifulle fayce and forme in y Lande. Hir ankulles wir full slim and slenderre, hir wayste trim and neat and she hadde also an magnificente payre of Bristolles. Many seeing hir, woldst fall strait in love with hir, evyn thoe she hadde y Allergick Dermatitisse (which oft broke owt after Strew-berries or Shell-fishe).

But, hir fathere, who Knew Notte Whatte Love Was, woldst fain discourage all hir sewters and boye-frendes, saying thus to all of them, 'Gette ye thine handes off of mie Daughterre, Sire Knyghte, or I shalle imprisonne thee in mie Dungeonne and do mannie Unpleasante thyngs to thyne Generatif Organnes with Tweezyres.' Thus did the Bewtifulle Princesse and hir superbe Bristolles know of noe manne his manhode. But thatte was the waye the coockie crumbelled oft tymes in those dayes.

Eventuallie, there arrived at y Castille a yonge Prince, bolde and fayre of fayce whoe stood highe in his Stirruppes (for twas sayed he was much troubelled by y Haemorrhoiddes, that menne oft calle y Pyles) and he gave showt to y Kynge insyde y Castille that hir was an Handsomme Prince who woldst marry y Princesse. From y Towre Mightie, replyde the Kynge, 'Many have per-sewed this course, Sire Knyghte, butte I Know Notte Whatte Love is, so sodde offe, or shall I calle y Fuzze!'

Quoth y Prince, 'Hang thou on anne minnitte! I woldst parlie with thee of love.' And, once insyde y Portcullis, spake he of Love and its mannie aspecks. He spake of y Byrds and y Bees and of Menne and Woemenne. And he shewed poemmes and sonnettes of Love and alsoe many diagrammes, some anatomick, some biologick and some just playne lewde, but jollie interestynge all y same. And yet stille did y Kynge protest he Knew Notte Whatte Love was. Then, in finale, didde Prince lept to his feet and pinninge y Kynge agaynst y Walle, putt his foote in y Kynge's Groyne sayinge: 'Eithere thou learnst what 'tis to love or else thous kisse thy Knuttes goodbye, O Snottie Gytte!'

Thenne, sayed y Kynge, 'I *doe* know now whatte Love is. And you *shalle* marrie mie daughterre. And since I know Love, shalle I command mie soldyres to laye doun thir Arms and shall all y Peopolle in y Countrie love one anotherre.'

And whenne thatte Proclammationne went forthe, did his soldyres laye doun thir Arms. And did the Enemies of y Kynge make Peace. Didde they Hell! They overrann y Castille Highe

'Eithere thou learnst
what 'tis to love or else
thou kisse thy Knuttes
goodbye.'

and Mightie and turned it into an Bingoe Halle with Two Licensed Barres and y Olde Worlde Grille Roome. And thus y Princesse was mayde to become an Barre-Mayde and y Peopolie came from many myles arounde to have them an jollie goode looke at hir superbe Bristolles.

MORALLE: One Swallow Doesn't Make Anne Summers.

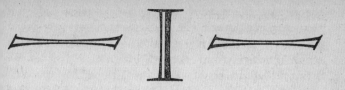

IDENTITY CRISIS

Doctors have fewer identity crises than other people. This is because every time a doctor asks himself the question 'Who am I?' he can look down at his left lapel, where a white oblong plastic name-badge tells him exactly who he is. When I was appointed to my very first job as a houseman, I was sent a form asking how I would like my name-badge engraved. Now up till then, I'd been simply Buckman RAA and no questions asked – and certainly no questions answered. But now, it seemed, the choice was almost limitless. I could style myself Dr Buckman, or Dr Robert Buckman, or Dr Buckman RAA, or Dr RAA Buckman.

My first choice was Dr R Buckman AA in the hope that my patients would think that I had the backing of the Automobile Association behind me in case of difficulties. Fortunately my friend Gerald pointed out in time that there was another organization whose initials were AA, and whose backing would not confer on its member the same degree of reliability and confidence. In the end I changed my name by deed poll to Barry Scylla Philip David Buckman, and had my badge engraved as Dr Buckman B. Sc. Ph. D.

Actually there was a student in our year from somewhere in the Philippines whose name was O. Phongprapatawanajala. (His friends called him Dick.) In the particular region he came from they never sounded the last six syllables of any proper names, so in his native tongue his name was pronounced Phongpra. He got so fed up explaining this to people that he snipped the last twelve letters off his name-badge and kept them in a drawer. The medical school were very slow to get used to this, and marked him down as 'absent' for the whole of his first year.

But the all-time champion of the name-badge war was my friend and colleague Rodney Taylor. When he got the form asking how he'd like his houseman's badge done, he asked them to engrave it 'The Man Standing Behind Me Is The Consultant'.

I think we doctors are terribly lucky to be carrying emblems of our identity around with us. It is, after all, a distinction we share with some of the finest and most skilled professions in the world – air hostesses, for instance. While we're on the subject, there is an old joke about an American airline that encouraged all its hostesses to wear badges announcing their first names. There was one hostess called Patricia who was extremely well developed around the balconies. Anyway, she duly perched her Patricia badge on the left side of her uniform and a drunk businessman stared at it for two minutes and said, 'Patricia. How cute! What do you call the right one?'

Despite the advantages of name-badges, there are times when it is very embarrassing to admit who you are. If you're caught breaking and entering, for example. The time that name-badges most embarrass me is when I attend a symposium or conference. Partly this is due to the fact that I'm nervous of making a fool of myself (see *Goofs*), but mainly it is due to the uneasy sensation I get when an unknown senior doctor stares at my left lapel while talking to me. It makes me twitch and shuffle my feet, and this often gives the other person the impression that I am an impostor. I see this idea creeping into their consciousness, and I immediately try to correct it by saying something to show that I am really a doctor after all. Of course by this time I'm so embarrassed and confused that what I do say sounds inept and stupid thus not only does it appear that I am not medically qualified, but it seems that I might actually be an escapee from Borstal. On one occasion I got so tied up that I said to the person who was trying to read my name: 'If I *had* escaped from Borstal, you don't think I'd come to a symposium on pharmacology, do you?' He suddenly developed an interest in the garden and hurried away. So did I, and didn't dare come back for the afternoon session, which is why I know so little about the side-effects of the newer aminoglycosides.

Even though I am immune from identity crises at work, I still suffer from them at other times. There is a great vogue for labelling car windscreens with white lettering stuck up at the top so you can read it from the outside. It seems customary to label both the left- and right-hand sides of the screen so that you can tell at a glance the name of the driver and his girl-friend. Round where I live there's a Dave-Freda (white Cortina), a Jimmy-Helen (black Escort) and two Mike-Tinas (one Mini and one Rolls Royce). It so happens that my next-door neighbour has done this to his car (a BMW), and his girlfriend is called Charlie. He gave me a lift to work the other week and I was so embarrassed to be sitting under a sign saying 'Charlie', next to the one saying 'John', that I rolled down the window and shouted, 'I'm not Charlie, I'm Robert.' Unfortunately this did not correct the impression that I was going steady with John; it merely suggested that we hadn't got round to changing the lettering yet.

(To tell the truth, what I really wanted to write about here was the silliness of some stickers that I've seen lately in the back windows of cars, constantly exhorting the public to Support Real Tennis, Free The Finchley Four, Make Cervical Smears An Olympic Event, Stop The Use of Words Ending In -ivity, et cetera. Oh well, some other time, perhaps.)

IRIDOLOGY

The basic idea of iridology is that you can tell what is wrong with any part of the body or mind simply by looking closely at the iris of the eye. It is a new fad in 'fringe medicine' about to invade us from America, and is the greatest crock of poo since palmistry.

Apparently this nonsense all started in the early 1800s with a man called Ignatz von Péczely (you think I'm kidding?) who found an owl and broke one of its legs (his story was that it was trying to escape). Anyway, he noticed a little black line in the bird's iris that disappeared when the leg got better. Little Ignatz later became a doctor, since in his native Hungary at that time all you needed to become a doctor was a good apprenticeship in breaking owls' legs. As a doctor, he began to look very closely at his patients' irises. Nowadays he would get some nice yellow tablets and occasional injections and he would be feeling much better in no time, but in those days this was the birth of a new science.

The central dogma of iridology is that every part of the body is represented in a different part of the iris like numbers round a clock face. If you look at any standard iridology chart (I got mine at Tesco's) you'll see that the thyroid gland is at half past nine in the left iris and at half past two in the right. Though of course it's an hour late during British Summer Time, a fact which obviously escaped von Péczely.

The kidney is at half past six which is just right as you get back from the office, but I was sorry to see that the vagina is at ten to seven which would certainly interfere with dinner.

The small intestines only begin at seven o'clock and are almost finished by a quarter to eleven, which would explain why they're always asleep for the Epilogue.

It seems the iris also develops 'stress rings' that show you when you've had too much stress. I saw a picture of a composer's eye reported as follows by an iridology doctor: 'The yellow shows congestion of the sinuses. But worse than this

man's badly pocketed intestines is his severe stress, indicated by four rings.'

Well, we modern-day doctors can understand stress and the badly pocketed intestine. In my opinion anyone even attempting to pocket his own intestines, however badly, would be subject to enormous stress (and indeed, mess) even to the extent of four rings (three rings, by the way, gets you Frou-Frou, the French model on the second floor). The only question I want to ask is which bit of the iris tells you that you've got something wrong with your iris. Answers on a postcard only, please.

However, I mustn't leave you with the idea that iridology is just a diagnostic aid; it can also *predict* the future! So my source assures me, 'Babies are now born with indications of degenerate conditions usually associated with old age. Their eyes reflect their parents' fiery stomachs, ballooning intestines and worn out colons.' I was so worried by this that I rushed up to look at my daughter's eyes. I must admit I did see a spot that might have been a reflection of my own fiery stomach, but I managed to get it out with a wisp of cotton wool. I trust that this means my daughter will now live to be ninety-four.

Well, I think that's all you need to know about iridology, but don't worry about it. We British doctors will never resort to looking at the iris of our patients' eyes to find out what's wrong with them, we'll read the tea leaves and the tarot cards as usual.

JARGON

Medical jargon is the verbal equivalent of the doctors' illegible handwriting. It prevents the patient from accidentally finding out what is wrong with him and, at the same time, often prevents the doctor from realizing that he doesn't know what *is* wrong with the patient.

The earliest form of jargon was simply to translate everything into Latin. The most common examples of this occur in dermatology. For instance if you see a red rash that spreads outwards in circles, you call it *erythema annulare centrifugum* and to hell with what's causing it. In fact, from an intellectual point of view, this is merely an adult form of train spotting. I remember when I was a casualty officer at St Nissen's a patient turned up and actually said that he had a red rash in circles that spread outwards and I looked at it and said, Aha! this is erythema annulare centrifugum, and he said what does that mean, and I said it means a red rash in circles that spread outwards, and he said but I just told *you* that, what are you a doctor or a parrot? I wrote out a prescription and said, rather haughtily, that I'd not met a parrot that could speak Latin, to which he replied that his parrot may not have been able to speak Latin but it had better handwriting than me and didn't cost the taxpayer a penny in fancy education. All of which goes to prove that when the Ancients tried to keep the diagnoses from their patients, they may have had their reasons.

Of course, keeping important information from the uninitiated has the disadvantage that most medical students tend to be fully paid-up members of the uninitiated. I remember one hectic afternoon when I was a student, during my first medical attachment, we had a very blustery chocks-away type of registrar on call. He wanted some blood tests done on a patient and dashed up to me and started blathering away. 'Get your notebook out, boy. Now that old dear in cubicle D – get an FBC and an ESR and diff., then a U and E, an SGOT, CPK and HBD and an Fe and TIBC.' To which I replied, 'Fine. And would you like mixed vegetables or just a green salad?' I can't bring myself to write down exactly what he said to me after that, but all I can say is that I didn't understand it either. I was too young. I still am. Anyway the upshot of that little *contretemps* with the registrar was that I was give a C minus for that medical attachment and the registrar later went on to do a five-year PhD in spelling.

Another way of keeping the jargon tight and cliquey is to use eponyms, e.g. Parkinson's disease, Cumurati-Engelmann disease or even Crigler-Najjar syndrome (all genuine). Now these are just the names of the people who first described the association of the various symptoms or signs.

For instance, if you happen to examine ten Czechoslovakian pipe fitters and you notice that they all have big blue blotches on their shins and complain of pain in their ears when they pass water, then you write a report about it in a medical journal. If your name is Fafner, let's say, (and it probably is) then that collection of bits and bobs is thenceforward called Fafner's syndrome, and soon everybody writes in to the medical journals to say they've seen similar cases. Then someone called, say, Fasolt writes in to say he's seen the same problems occuring in Hungarian hockey players and is this a hitherto unsuspected sub-variant? Then everybody calls it Fasolt-Fafner syndrome until somebody else writes in to say that it all gets better with Milk of Magnesia and calamine lotion and that it's really all due to 'flu, with the blue blotches caused by the dye running from their overalls. Then, two years later, the daily press gets hold of it and says BRITISH DOCTORS MAJOR BREAKTHROUGH IN FOREIGN KILLER DISEASE, and we're all ready to start afresh on something else.

However, to be perfectly fair, it's not the doctors who are the worst offenders in the matter of jargon. I think ambulance crews are even worse. Let me say in fairness to them that they really do heroes' work and without their support and help many a fancy casualty officer (e.g. me) would have given up long ago. But in all the excitement, ambulance crews tend to slip into a sort of Biggin Hill jargon and say things like, 'We got a one-five from Romeo Bravo and brought in a suspended query OD from Central on a blue without the two-tone.'

One winter there was a spate of terrorist activity in London and an ambulanceman rushed up to me and said. 'There's been an Echo Delta in Oxford Street.' There was a very long pause while I looked at him trying to guess what an Echo Delta might be, but eventually I gave up and broke the inviolable code of jargon by asking what the hell it was, anyway. The ambulanceman explained very slowly, as if to a child, that Echo Delta was the call sign for ED, and that the initials ED stood for Explosive Device. There was another long pause and then I asked did that mean a bomb, and he said, well yes, now I came to mention it, that's exactly what it meant. So I said if they meant a bomb and had to give it some fancy bloody call-sign, why didn't they call it a Bertie Orange Mother Bertie and have done with it? And the ambulanceman said that wasn't the way they did it at Central and why didn't I just Percy India Sugar Sugar off?

As I say, if you're not in with the jargon you're out. Over and out.

JAUNDICE

Jaundice is a funny thing. It makes the whites of the eyes go yellow which is much more disturbing if you're well acquainted with the victim before the onset of the jaundice. This point was made very forcibly for me when my colleague and confrère Beetles developed hepatitis. (He said he'd caught it from a lavatory seat, but we know better, don't we, children?) I suppose that I had expected him to look vaguely Chinese, but in fact, compared to his previous appearance, he just looked rather shoddy and more sort of made in Hong Kong than genuinely Chinese. I just thought you'd like to know, that's all.

KILDARE

See *TV Doctors*

KIPLING

I was at a very smart cocktail party recently and found myself talking to a bloke who was 'in advertising'. I told him I was thinking of writing a book (this was before I discovered how to do it *without* thinking, of course) and he said, 'I've got one piece of advice for you: go up-market.' I didn't find this particularly encouraging, since it conjured up visions of schlapping down the Liverpool Road with a sackload of vegetables; which may be okay for the Harold Pinters of this world, but if you've spent seven years in medical training, then as a pastime it rates slightly below suicide. I mentioned this to my brother, who is himself a famous author, and he said I had misunderstood the vernacular. Or words to that effect.

'Up-market' is Harrods and Rolls-Royce, 'down-market' (according to those in the know) is *Crossroads*, greyhound racing, and the Dansette 'Bermuda' (my first gramophone). Anyway, I took this advertising man's advice quite seriously and if you've been unable to spot the up-market sections of the book so far, I'll give you a clue: there haven't been any. I shall now remedy this by moving swiftly into an investigation of the role of illness in the creation of our cultural heritage.

Take Rudyard Kipling, for instance. According to my sources (the Lancet 'Supplement of Spurious Biography'), Rudyard was fairly ill all his life. In fact, to quote Professor Ernst Broacher, 'Rudyard regarded his life from the age of seven and a half to fifty-one as merely a prolonged convalescence.' The crucial period of his life was when, at the age of six, he was admitted to Saint Ear Nose and Throat's Hospital for a tonsillectomy. Separated from his brother John and his father Dad, little Rudyard was subject to fits of depression and moodiness. After the tonsillectomy he had feelings of profound neglect and rejection – apparently they threw away the wrong bit. However there were compensations: while in hospital he came under the influence of two of his favourite childhood fancies – ice cream, and nurses in black stockings.

If I may quote from Donald Isselbacher's monograph *The Influence of the Sinusitis on Victorian Poetry* (and why shouldn't I?) ... 'the influence of ice cream and nurses in black stockings on Kipling's poetical maturation can hardly be over-emphasized'. In fact it can hardly be mentioned at all. Later in life, the adult Kipling would recall those happy times and capriciously demand a dozen ice creams and two dozen nurses in black stockings. It was in such a mood of retrospective indulgence that he wrote his prodigious poem 'The Song of the Out-Patients'.

One could hardly do better than reproduce that little-known poem here (if, by the way, you think that one *can* do better, please don't hesitate to tell one):

> Shall I revisit hospital
> And carefree days gone by?
> I'll not forgo what I've forgot,
> For go I'll not, not I!

Long the moaning, long the aching,
Long the lines of patients ranked
With throats from which the tonsils
Have been so rudely yanked.

I never want to see you more
Your ward my soul avoids,
Wherein I left so much behind
(They're called my adenoids).

But yet I *would* return to you,
Forgive your grim black side,
And see that little staff nurse
With the really neat backside.

By gosh, she did have lovely legs
That ran at our behest:
Her uniform could scarce contain
That boundless bouncy chest.

And when she dropped her scissors
And stooped, those stockings black
Gave Higgins in bed twenty-three
His seventh heart attack.

Came the dawning, came the day-staff,
Came the grey and chilly tea.
Came that timid blanket-bather
Always left some bits to me.

Shall I go back to that dread place?
I'd rather drop down dead!
I think I'll ring that staff nurse
And bring her here instead.

You have just been up-market. And don't say I didn't warn
you.

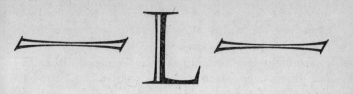

LANGUAGE

Around St Nissen's there is a large Italian population, that is to say a population of large Italians. This would never have bothered me except that when I was a medical student I somehow acquired a reputation for being able to speak Italian. I decided to treat this reputation as I would have treated a reputation for extraordinary sexual prowess – I left it alone (not wanting to dispel it altogether) and hoped that it would never be tested. Unfortunately, one day it was tested, weighed in the balance and found absent without leave.

Our group had just been assigned to obstetrics, and it was on our very first day on the Labour Ward while we were all huddled together in the middle feeling very raw and shifting nervously from foot to foot and whistling. The obstetric registrar rushed up and asked which one of us was the Italian translator. It seemed that a certain Signora Rosalino was well advanced in labour, and no one knew the Italian for 'the cervix is fully dilated'.

I was whisked down the corridor, and pushed into the Labour Room where la Signora lay in waiting. She was one of those enormous placid Madonna types who looked as if her father was a gigolo and her mother a Guernsey. She was lying on her back with her legs in stirrups in a position then unknown to me, but now recognized (and indeed revered) as the lithotomy position. However, at the time I found it very damaging to my naïve sense of social propriety, and so, despite the fact that I had been taught always to shake hands with my patients at the beginning of any interview, I just sort of stared at the ground and went very red.

The registrar pushed in behind me and said that since I was meant to be learning obstetrics why didn't I put on a surgical glove and feel the baby's head. I found a glove and then, very gingerly, I felt the baby's head, trying to remember what I'd been told about the position it was in. Halfway through this, my sense of *politesse* and rectitude suddenly overcame me, and I came over all coy and embarrassed about doing this to a patient to whom I hadn't even said good morning. Since my right hand was intimately involved in the nether regions, I was rather handicapped, and didn't dare to try a left-handed handshake from where I was standing; so I compromised and, waving at her in a rather half-hearted fashion with my free hand. I said, '*Ciao!*'

Given the circumstances this was probably a bit too informal and the registrar was very quick to point this out. It was a very bad start. I stopped my examination of the baby and the registrar said that anyway la Signora was in the second stage of labour and would I tell her that, please. I had a bash.

'*Il dottore a detto,*' I said,' *che questo e la secundo piano di lavoro, e pronto la bambino va la.*' ('The doctor has said that this is the second storey of a factory and soon your son, she will go there.')

The Signora stared at me in frank disbelief and then took a good long suck at the nitrous oxide. The registrar started getting impatient, 'Tell her the neck of the womb is fully dilated.'

'Right,' I said, trying desperately to remember whether neck was '*collo*' or '*collino*'. I chose blindly. '*La collina de la vostro* ... er ... *istero e aperto Totallmente.*' ('The hillock of your madness is open. 'Totally.') She took three very long sucks at the nitrous oxide, which fortunately rendered her almost unconscious, and they took advantage of the temporary calm to shove her on to a trolley and wheel her into the Delivery Room.

In the Delivery Room things took a more dramatic turn. The midwife scrubbed and gowned and looked very intimidating indeed. (Actually, later on I came to know this particular midwife very well. As did the rest of the medical school. But that's another story.) 'Get this lady to push! Tell her to push – NOW!' the midwife yelled. I panicked and the last remnants of my Linguaphone deserted me. '*Tirez!*' I said. This was not Italian for 'push', but French for 'pull'. La Signora was in no position to pull anything, least of all the head of her unborn child. The midwife pointed out my error very loudly, and with little restraint.

The registrar returned from his quiet fag, checked the baby's position and told me to tell the mother that he would have to use the obstetric forceps. '*Questo,*' I said, touching the forceps (which were unfortunately sterile and had to be replaced *subito*), '*questo e la forcipessa.*' This meant nothing at all. '*E come un cuchiaillo por la testa di bambino.*' ('It is like a spoon for the baby's head.') This gave la Signora the idea that her baby would only walk with his head in spoons.

Ignoring the mother's uncomprehending panic, the registrar applied the forceps and the midwife shrieked at me, 'Get her to push. TO PUSH! PUSH!' I went to pieces and my mind floated back to my memories of the car train to Rome with those tri-lingual instructions printed under the windows. '*E PERICOLOSO SPORGERSI!*' I yelled. This means: 'It is dangerous to lean out.'

I couldn't believe what I'd just said. The mother was lying there looking at a sweaty medical student shouting at her baby – in Italian – that it was dangerous to lean out. What could *he* know about the world that she didn't? She drew breath to swear at me – and reflexly pushed. And her son was born. Everyone burst into tears and I tried to wish the baby Happy Birthday. Apparently I wished him a Prosperous

New Year, but by that time nobody gave a twopenny stuff what I said. And quite right, too.

LIBRARIES

Being of a bookish nature and rather slight, not to say stunted, I've always been struck by libraries. No that's not quite true – I've always been struck in libraries. Anyway I've always thought that libraries had a universal sort of authoritarian air, like the Salvation Army, say, or the Women's Institute. It therefore came as a surprise to me when I visited Cornwall and found a strange tribe of country folk who had never seen twentieth-century civilization (well, not since the Saturday before, anyway). They were a gang of desperados, cut-throats and pirates, in a region where it was quite normal to run away to sea. Two years earlier a mobile library had visited the neighbourhood and these pirates were so struck by the rakish devil-may-care attitude of the staff, that they wrote a song glorifying the carefree life of the librarian and warning their young folk off it.

I reproduce it here solely as a service to the memory of Cecil Sharpe because he missed it. For those that like to sing, the chorus tune is a bit like the Roger de Coverley (but not very much), and should be sung with one hand cupped over the left ear (to stop the wax falling out on the high notes):

> When I was just a wee bonny boy,
> My father said to me
> You can do what you like when you're older, son,
> You can run away to sea,
> You can rob and steal, or fight abroad
> For thunder and gloree-o,
> But you'll break your mother's heart
> On the day that you start
> To work for the libraree. O!

The librar-ee! The librar-ee!
The only place I want to be.
They've give me my ticket
So I know I'll have to stick it,
And stay with the library.

There's Nabokov, Goncharov, Borges and Burgess,
Alvarez and Huxley and E. Allan Poe.
A slim one by Auden, the tales of Flash Gordon,
Teach Yourself Maths and the Story of O. Oh!
There's Croce on Ethics, and Pevsner on Sussex,
Essex on sex, Germaine Greer on her own.
There's Howard and Coward on Karma and Drama,
There's Amis who's famis and always on loan.

My mother cried that she wished I'd died
Before I'd done this thing. Ing!
I'd be the shame of my family name
Through the whole of Godalming. Ing!
If I'd only done what my father done.
He never did a bloody thing-o;
Hobbing and a-nobbing and a-on-the-jobbing,
And always playing bing-o.

The librar-ee! The librar-ee!
The only place I want to be.
I've wined and I've dined
But I'd rather be fined
Found at the library.

There's Leacock and Peacock and A. Solzhenitsyn,
There's Ordinance maps of the old Cheddar Gorge,
There's bed-sitter guides for the lady who eats in,
There's Eliot T. S., and Eliot George.
There's Tropic of Cancer (a randy bonanza),
Fleming and Hemingway, Dante and Kant,
There's Bligh on 'the Bounty', Cartland on County
And 'Learning the Can-Can' for people who can't.

I'll take my knapsack off my back
And shake the salt from my hair-o,
When the wind whistles free through the main-mast tree

Thank God I won't be there-o.
With my little rubber stamp and my catalogue
Of cards of green and white, I'll
Re-arrange the lot, to show what we've got
By author and by title.

The librar-ee! The librar-ee!
The only place I want to be.
I got the cramp
From my little rubber stamp
Down at the library.

There's Montaigne and Fontaine and Cato and Plato,
There's Melly and Shelley and Byron and Keats,
There's 'Grow Your Own Cactus, Bamboo or Potato',
There's books on great massacres, routs and defeats.
There's Carroll on hattery, Austen on flattery,
Thousands of biogs of Strausses and Bachs,
There's Gray on Anatomy (what can grey matter be?)
Lenin on lamp-posts and K. Marx and Sparks.

The librar-ee! The librar-ee!
The only place I want to be be.
I get my smiles
From a night on the files,
Down at the library.

CHORUS
OH! Roger de Coverley, Roger de Coverley,
He polished up that knocker so carefully
Fol-de-lol dol! Hey nonny hoo-hah!

MASOCHISTS

Masochists are people who get pleasure from pain or abuse and after my ten years experience of the National Health Service it is my belief that every doctor is one (or maybe several).

There was never any doubt in my mind that I should become a doctor (see *Ambition*), since all my family are masochists, my father being the most blatant. He used to be very keen on physical fitness and on learning French irregular verbs – both activities being, in their own way, painful and abusive. He found a way to combine the two; he wrote his French irregular verbs in red crayon on shirt cardboard and leant them upside down against the wall at one end of the bathroom. He then stripped naked and did a handspring against the door at the other end, shouting out his verbs while pressing himself up and down on his hands. I'm told he did this for years before I was born – in fact it's a miracle I was born at all. Anyway, doing press-ups on your hands makes you grunt: actually you perform what is known as the Valsalva manoeuvre which does no end of damage to your French diction. As it happens, in my father's case, it made no difference as we found out when we heard him speaking French the right way up.

The first I knew about my father's curious aberration was when I was eight years old and I walked past the bathroom in the early morning and heard these highly unusual sounds of his Valsalva in French, or French in Valsalva. It sounded like: *Jerr-swerr-twerr-erhh-illnhh-errhhnn*. Hearing the word 'ill' I rushed in, thrusting open the door against which my father was doing his handstand and dealing him a near-lethal blow to the kidneys from the door-knob. I was thus greeted with the sight of my venerated parent grovelling on the floor, his face a deep purply-red (having been upside down for ten minutes) and his genitals a pallid grey. This made a big impression on my eight-year-old mind and it wasn't until I was medically qualified that I realized that the reverse is the usual state of affairs. Still, the incident didn't put me off exercise, or French or nudity, but I've never felt the same about shirt cardboard since.

After that experience I decided to become a doctor, and Dad went on to develop sciatica. When he explained to the specialist what he did behind the bathroom door, the specialist gave him a course of phenylbutazone, a steel corset, and a set of French Linguaphone records. All of them came in useful, though he still speaks French as if he was standing on his hands. He has since given up handsprings and taken up learning Mandarin Chinese from records, and such is his uncanny ability with foreign languages that many of his Chinese friends on hearing him order meals in a Chinese restaurant think he is talking French.

Anyway it's my belief that most doctors are masochists. I mean look at how they remember their houseman years – with immense nostalgia. Most of us at this stage of our careers spent nights of quivering terror when we had to look at hundreds of yards of ECG tracings and dozens of chest x-rays with our reddened, sleepless eyes; and we felt sea-sick around the knees as we wondered whether to call the registrar out of bed again. We must have clocked up at least a hundred hours a week and got emotionally involved with our patients' problems and pains, and received regular drubbings and only occasional congratulations from our consultants as we tried to make up for our ignorance with sweat and toil and maybe even tears. And we did all that, and we

PALLEZ VOUS FLANCAIS?

were proud of and we loved it; or rather we hated it and loved hating it. Which is the same thing.

And why do we do it all? Because we're masochists. It's not the work load that reduces doctors to gibbering whingeing wrecks; it is the lack of appreciation. I believe that if we were treated with a mixture of filial obedience, servile gratitude and mildly sycophantic reverence, most of us would work until comatose.

In fact this forms the basis of my plan to right the wrongs of the NHS. I would employ two hundred actors whom I would train to imitate heart failure. In strict rotation they would ring up every doctor in the country at three o'clock in the morning. When the doctor arrived, whatever treatment he gave would cause instantaneous relief of symptoms. The patient would then shake the doctor's hand and (in certain circumstances) kiss it or weep over it. After the doctor had left, the patient would write a letter to the Community Health Council praising him, and ten days later another actor, pretending to be the chairman of the council, would call on the doctor, show the letter and thank him on behalf of a grateful community. This service would cost about £15 million to start with, but in terms of reduced wranglings and increased productivity, would pay for itself in about twenty minutes.

Which reminds me, may I take this opportunity of saying how much we in the hospital service appreciate the dedication, self-denial and efforts of our colleagues, the public. You're all doing a grand job and if you're reading this book while waiting in an Out-Patient clinic, you've got another fifty pages to go before the doctor will be ready to see you.

Deep down inside, most doctors have a nagging suspicion that they are grossly ignorant, and that modern medicine, however shiny and glossy, is really only one step ahead of the witch doctor and magician. For that reason it is very comforting to root around in the history books and find idiocies of past ages to bolster our egos. My own personal comfort is a book called *The Masterpiece*. It is attributed to Aristotle but is probably a rag-bag compiled over two or three hundred years using Aristotle and Marcus Antonius Zimaras Sanctipertias (you remember him, don't you?) among others. The whole of the first part of the book is a guide to midwifery and gynaecology, and apparently it had a wide circulation below stairs where it was considered Pretty Racy Stuff. However, the second part is a fascinating question and answer routine which is somewhat erratic in its accuracy.

For instance, it revives the idea that the brain is the organ that cools the blood. This misconception was current in Aristotle's day, the basic concept being that the brain acted like a radiator (which is why it looked all folded up, see?) and as the blood ran over it, the brain purged it of the watery humours which were expelled through the nose. Hence the following question:

Q: Why doth the nose stand out farther than any other part of the body?

A: Because the nose is, as it were, the sink of the brain, by which the phlegm of the brain is purged; and therefore it doth stand forth, lest the other parts be defiled.

This should have comforted anyone in Grecian days who wanted to take a pocket hanky and blow their brains out; at least the nose would keep the brains clear of the shirt front.

For the most part, the questions were answered in what is now known as Aristotelean style – 'things are the way they are because that's the way they're meant to be'. Hence:

Q: Why have we two eyes and but one nose?
A: Because that light is more necessary to us than smelling.

And jolly lucky, too. Otherwise of course we'd be unable to smell in the dark, would go blind when we had a cold, and would spend Saturday afternoons in front of the television, sniffing the football.

However some of the replies were pure nonsense, and for total incomprehensibility remained unsurpassed until the re-organization of the National Health Service in 1974. Viz:

Q: Why are not women bald?
A: Because they are cold and moist – for moistness doth give nutriment to the hair, and coldness doth bind the pores.

And if you don't believe it, take a cold moist woman up to your room, keep her warm and dry and see if her hair falls out.

NATIONAL HEALTH SERVICE (ADVT)

There seems to be one aspect of the National Health Service that has received far too little attention; as well as being a service, and as well as being a service concerned with health, it is also a nationalized industry. This means that we can justifiably examine the NHS in the same way that we look at other nationalized industries, e.g. the Post Office, Gas Board, Electricity Board and Steel Industry.

In fact, all these industries have a great deal in common with the NHS – they all employ lots of workers in white coats and, at any one time, half their work force is in hospital. I would even go so far as to say that it is becoming increasingly difficult to distinguish between a crowded Post Office and an Out-Patient Clinic; they rank equal on cleanliness, delay, amount of coughing and age of posters on the wall. This actually gives rise to the famous nationalized industries riddle which runs as follows:

Q: How do you tell a Post Office from an Out Patients Department?

A: I don't know.

Q: Well that's the last time I send *you* out to get your hernia repaired.

You may be wondering what all this is leading up to. I know I am. So, let's all read on together and find out, eh?

Basically the chief difference between the NHS and the

other nationalized industries is that they are all allowed to advertise themselves and we are not.

I'm sure you know what I'm talking about. There are those long adverts in the cinema showing how electricity can cook toast and work electric razors, and equally long ones showing how gas cookers work better on gas. (Better than on what? Sea-dredged aggregates? Marijuana?) Now ask yourselves this: how much does this cost the nation? Now ask yourselves this: *why* did you just ask yourselves how much does this cost the nation? You don't know, do you? That's the trouble with you reading public, you're always asking yourselves things you don't know the answer to, instead of asking the people who do, i.e. your doctor.

Speaking as a doctor, I can tell you that this advertising costs the nation £350 million a year. No, sorry, £145,000 million a year. (You'll find you don't need to be more accurate than that with the nationalized industries – see *Industry, Steel*). I'm not the first one to bring this horrendous expenditure into the open. In 1976, the Electricity Board got a lot of stick for their huge advertising budget and they got very huffy about it. They said, look here, okay, we're a nationalized industry but we're still in competition with other sources of power, e.g. gas and butane. (They obviously felt safe from threats by solar cells, tidal power and chicken manure gas.)

Now just think what they're implying. At the time of writing, the daily papers are carrying a full page advert showing a huge traffic jam with the headline 'Where would you be without traffic lights? Think Electric!' What can this mean? Do the Electricity Board think that the Gas Boards are trying to flog a new line of gas-powered traffic lights? Are we in for a new series of adverts like:

'I always prefer stopping at an *electric* traffic light – you get a smoother pull-away from the green and, of course, there's no smell.'

And if competition is the *raison d'être* of the Electricity Board's adverts, then what about those cinema ones I mentioned. How many of us were about to rush out and buy a gas-powered electric razor? Or a butane powered one? (Actually, I have just thought of someone who shaves with butane. Desperate Dan, but then he uses a blow torch.) And as for lighting, ha! Are the Electricity Board seriously suggesting that there are millions of people sitting at home, turning up their gas mantles, and saying:

'Goodness gracious, apparently there's this stuff called electricity that we could be using for our lighting. Isn't it lucky they've spent a trillion pounds advertising it, otherwise we'd never have heard of it. Let's pop round to the showroom this very minute and hire a box of it.'

And the same applies to the Post Office. All those telly ads telling you to use the phone. As opposed to what exactly? Semaphore? Throwing up the window and shouting? (Don't say letters because that's the Post Office, too.) To be fair there are some occasions when you *do* want to use some other method of communication. If you happen to be Queen of England and it's your Silver Jubilee, for instance, you might think it a nice idea to light a chain of beacon fires covering the whole country. But don't tell me our Queen had second thoughts the night before she lit them and said, Oh dear, maybe we should call it all off, I saw this advert on the telly that says we should use the phone. (It's just occurred to me that maybe she *did* say that and then realized that she didn't have fifty-two million tuppenny bits.)

My whole point is that there is *no justifiable reason whatsoever* for the nationalized industries to indulge in advertising, and therefore, since they all do, the National Health Service ought to be doing it, too. Fair's fair. It just so happens that I've got a few nice ideas for adverts for the NHS, and thought you might like a little preview.

(*soft music*) 'If you're going to be *really* ill, have you

thought about coming to hospital? Of course you can try the greengrocers or the shoe shop, but we think you'll find that they haven't got as many nurses as *we* have. So come to St Nissen's – we're glad to see you so ill.'

OR:

(*Hup-tiddley music*) 'What's that? Pain in the right side of your tummy? Could be your gall bladder! If you're thinking of having it removed, let a doctor do it. The milkman, the electrician or even the (*wry chuckle*) bus conductor may want to have a crack at it for you – but our advice is, come to St Nissen's. You'll get your health – and we'll get *you*.'

My projected advertising budget for the NHS is a mere £120 million. Used notes only, please.

OBSTETRICS (HOME SECTION)

I've always been a scientific sort of chap, objective and cool in my judgements. So when my first child was born – four months ago, as a matter of fact – I didn't behave like most of your stupid boastful dads and start prattling on that it was the most beautiful baby in the world. Not me, no sirree. I asked the midwife. And the midwife said it was the most beautiful baby in the world; and let's face it, she must have seen thousands so I feel that I can pass the information on to you as a proven objective truth.

Not that I was surprised. At the ante-natal clinic at the five months stage they'd taken these pictures of our baby inside the womb with the ultrasound. As I've been trained in ultrasound pictures of the heart, I had a look at these for myself. I could see straight away that our baby had a normal head (bi-parietal diameter 6 cm), a normal heart (5 cm), and a penis 12.2 cm in length. This was a worry. Should I change my mind about putting his name down for Harrow? Would he get too much ragging in the showers? And who should do the circumcision? – Taylor Woodrow? Or should I put it out for tender? Well, since I'm an objective sort of a chap, I dealt with these problems at the highest level of hypo-thetico-deductive logic; that is to say, I ignored them. Other people call it lateral thinking, but with me it's the only way there is.

Now I don't want to go into details of the delivery – actu-ally I do, but it isn't the same without the hand gestures –

but I'd been well prepared for it by my tutors in obstetrics when I was a student, and by the elders of my tribe ever since. The process of labour is divided up into four distinct stages. Stage One is reached when the neck of the womb is 100% dilated (though my great-uncle said he could get 94% for wholesale). Stage Two is the delivery of the baby (at no extra charge anywhere within a ten centimetre radius). Stage Three is the delivery of the after-birth (a bit like the invoice, really), and Stage Four consists of telephoning the relatives (which is why I had to attend all those classes about breathing control).

In fact the birth itself was a great success all round – both the midwife and I found it to be a rewarding and emotionally enriching experience. I must say I couldn't understand why my wife insisted on all that puffing and grunting instead of getting rewarded and emotionally enriched as well. Incidentally, if any of you are considering becoming fathers in the near future, you should be warned about something called the Transition Stage. As the cervix becomes dilated fully, there is a surge of impulses up the nerves from the pelvis. This upsets a very subtle emotional balance and produces some very odd behaviour. One of the ladies at our breathing class had apparently sat up at this point, with contractions coming every ninety seconds, and said to her husband: 'Please let me go home now. I promise I'll come back tomorrow and finish off; but I'd like to go home now.'

My wife didn't say anything as daffy as that – oh no! Being the wife of an objective sort of chap, she was too busy singing 'Old MacDonald Had a Farm' with me. We'd selected that as our song for when the contractions got very heavy, as my wife couldn't sing anything more melodic than that at the best of times. As it was, the nitrous oxide/oxygen mixture seemed to make her slightly drunk and the last verse became somewhat drawn out: 'And on that farm he had some ... er ... cupboards.' (Long pause while she tried to work out what noise cupboards would make) 'With a ...

'I KNOW IT'S BEEN VANDALIZED...I'M JUST LOOKING FOR NAMES FOR THE BABY!'

chip chip ... here and a ... hmmph ... block block there.'
(They were obviously chipboard cupboards with block-
board doors – nothing but the best for our child.)

After a lot of rewarding and enriching pushing, the baby
was born. And I noticed straight away that my ultra-
sonically diagnosed son had chosen to be born a girl. I think
this showed admirable diplomacy since 81% of the tribe
didn't like the name we'd chosen – Roderick – which is a
pretty silly name for a girl anyway.

Now I learnt all about the development of the foetus
when we did embryology at medical school, and I knew how
the baby develops from a thing called a blastocoele with
things called neural crests that invaginate and so on; but it
meant nothing at that moment. As I stood there, with
scientific and objective tears rolling down my cheeks, my
only thought was 'good gracious it must have taken them
years to get these fingernails done so perfectly'. Despite all
my training and knowledge, Gremlinology took over instantly. My mind filled with visions of thousands of tiny little
intra-uterine Japanese engineers building my daughter
('twelve functions as a chronograph, ten functions as a stop-
watch and two functions as an alimentary canal'). Her ears
were flattened against her temples and I sort of expected to
see a little sign saying: 'Loosen transit screws before use to
allow ears free movement'. And as we sat there in the delivery room, amid the bloody effluvia and the disposables,
the sun streamed in and our daughter started chuckling. I'm
telling you it was better than sex or, as they say nowadays,
better than hang-gliding. (For those that don't know the
difference, the former is associated with fewer broken ankles.
Except in Australia – a fact that I *can* explain but don't
want to now.)

I see now that a huge part of my life ended then. I became
a different man. From now on, I won't be able to see shots of
babies as in *The Ten Commandments* or *Gone With The
Wind* without getting lumpy around the throat. I'll be

worried about traffic and about men in raincoats. In other words, I'm in the Big Swim; and about time, too. Of course, looking at it objectively (as I always do) I realize that if some victim of society in sixteen years time strives for a meaningful relationship and happens to involve my daughter in emotional or even physical trauma, then I, as a comprehending and tolerant member of that society, will chop his head off.

PHYSICAL FITNESS – (A DOCTOR WRITES)

Many patients ask their doctor what exercise they should be doing to get physically fit. It would be much better if before going to their doctor the patients asked themselves (a) what am I trying to get fit for? and (b) what was I fit for before I became unfit and started trying to get fit for whatever I'm trying to get fit for now? This would probably take all day and most patients would never actually get to their doctor.

The important issue here is that some people are born to be short and stocky, some are born to be tall and lanky, and some in between. It is obviously vital to know what you are at the outset so that, if you are four foot six and weigh eighteen stone, say, you don't waste time training to be a pole vaulter. (In fact, if you *are* four foot six and weigh eighteen stone you probably haven't *got* much time.) So how do you find out what kind of body you have been saddled with?

Well, you will be relieved to hear that there are only three basic kinds of body shape (or somatotype, as it is called), and everybody in the whole world is some combination of one or more of the three basic ingredients. The man who worked this system out in detail was named Sheldon, of Harvard, and he divided the entire human race into three groups (no mean task, it took him most of the afternoon) called the ectomorphs, the mesomorphs and the endomorphs. Put simply, the ectomorph has lots of skin in proportion to his muscle bulk and is therefore tall and lean. The mesomorph has a predominately muscular frame and is shorter and thicker, while the endomorph is short and squat with the emphasis very much on the belly.

Now to decide what kind you are, you simply look at yourself in the mirror (after taking your clothes off) and score each of these three ingredients on a scale of 1 to 9. (It used to be 1 to 7, but I think 1 to 9 gives us a bit more scope.) Allow me to illustrate.

If you are all skin and bones you score 911, and you're an ectomorph. You are between 5 ft 10 in and 6 ft 3 in (depending on the thickness of your socks) and your arm span is 5 ft 8 in, which makes you a poor second to the Golden Eagle. In cold weather you will need more carbohydrate because of your height and surface area, and in hot climates natives will hoist the Union Jack up your left leg at dawn. Your lucky number is eight, as is your hat size, your golf handicap and IQ. Your name is Raymond Phipps and if you leave the money in the usual place, I'll destroy the negatives. Once you are physically fit, you will be a good long-distance runner, pole vaulter or billiard cue.

If you score yourself 191, this makes you a mesomorph. You are thick-set and built with the kind of great British craftmanship that has given our garden furniture the reputation it deserves. You tend to prefer competitive games to cultural activities, your favourite colour is red and your favourite singer Joe Bugner. Why not go and look inside a health food shop? Then, once you've seen the prices, you'll probably want to go and open your own health food shop. This will make you not only a fit and trim mesomorph, but also a rich and sleek mesomorph, and, of all the somatotypes, the mesomorph looks best in fast shiny cars.

If you scored 119, you are an endomorph. You probably have a virile, rippling set of intestines and a huge pair of adrenals that you can frighten skinny weaklings on the beach with. You enjoy your food and, on good days, enjoy everyone else's as well. You are placid, difficult to rouse, easily satisfied and incompetent – you usually work for the

Gas Board. Endomorphs make good television critics and cushions.

If you score 111, you have far too little of everything. You are probably a picomorph, i.e. a weed. A fit picomorph has very pale skin, pink eyes, long ears and a waffly nose. If you are actually breathing you are a rabbit; if you are not breathing and your eyes are made of glass, then you are a novelty zip-up pyjama case.

If you have scored 999 you are probably a fire engine. You make a lot of noise and are handy to have around the house just in case.

As for myself, I score 226 – lacking in all physical attributes recognizable as human. However, since 226 is also my post code, it enables the Post Office to save money by sticking my letters straight into my mouth. A Doctor Has Written.

PHYSICS

A diligent study of physics is an essential prerequisite for any modern scientist, and the doctor is no exception. Unfortunately many doctors have only a very hazy idea of the basics of physics and it is for their benefit that I here append the answers to the three commonest problems of nuclear physics and the Special Theory of Relativity:

Q: Why can't you travel faster than light?
A: You can, but its always dark when you get there.

Q: What is the main advantage of the so-called 'electron clock' that works on the resonance spectrum of the rubidium atom?
A: You don't have to wind it.

Q: Why can't you have any particles smaller than electrons?
A: You can, it's just that they're out of stock at the moment.

There, now that's settled maybe we can get back to medicine.

QUERY NATURE

'Query nature' is a euphemism for 'I don't know'. For instance, if you're looking at a chest x-ray and you see a shadow that you think is pneumonia you might say, 'Opacity in right middle lobe query pneumonia'; but if you've got no idea what the hell it is, instead of saying so you can disguise your ignorance by describing as much as you can, and ending with 'query nature'.

My friend Derek took to 'query nature' like a delinquent to an air gun. He used it everywhere. When we were medical students confronted with curious x-rays, most of us would fumpher our way along saying things like, 'Gosh, well . . . um . . . this is . . . what the hell is this . . . etc.' But old Derek would call out from the back of the group, 'Radioluceny upper third of tibia query nature.' 'Query nature' became his soubriquet and it was always used with a certain degree of respect, until one night three months after he'd qualified.

He admitted a young girl to the medical ward with moderately severe asthma. It was three o'clock in the morning (it always is on such occasions), and Derek was not at his best when the chest x-ray arrived on the ward. At the top of each lung there were vertical shadows of a very curious shape. Query nature, in fact. Now Derek's consultant was the kind of chap who likes to be *involved*, and the usual rule is that, when a consultant says he wants to be called in for any problem no matter how small, you say, yes sir, and do nothing of the kind. Not if you want to stay in your job, you don't.

Anyway, Derek stared at these damned shadows for half an hour and then rang up his consultant and reported 'bilateral upper zone opacities, vertically disposed and somewhat patchy in distribution'. The boss said what are they, and Derek said query nature, sir, and the boss said right I'm coming in. He came in, looked at the x-ray and at the young girl, and said, 'Those are her pigtails, you fool.' And so they were. Hanging down behind her shoulders they'd caused the shadows on the x-ray.

Like most stories of this kind, this one got round the hospital quicker than cholera; although the effect on Derek was somewhat similar. Like an H. M. Bateman cartoon (you know the sort of thing: 'The Man Who Broke Wind in the Reading Room of the British Museum'), overnight Derek became the Man Who Called In His Boss To Look At Pigtails. By jove, there was some ragging from the chaps – offers of a drink came thick and fast: 'What's yours, Derek? – Sorry, I mean, drink query nature?' His food was 'pie query nature', his transport home was 'bus query nature' and so on. I'm told that a few years later he gave up medicine and went into politics. I think he should do very well. Don't you?

QUESTIONNAIRES

In our second pre-clinical year we had to take a pathology exam. It so happened that we were the first group to be subjected to this exam in questionnaire form. There would be a set of five horribly complicated statements followed by the question: How many of these statements are true? – (a) all of the above (b) none of the above (c) 1 and 3 but not 2 (d) 2 and 3 but not 1, and so on.

My colleague Dizzy Bernstein was the first to crack. After twenty minutes, he tore up his paper and gave the pieces to (or rather threw the pieces at) the invigilator, together with

the encouragement to return said fragments to the backside of the stupid sod who invented bloody questionnaires. (I should point out that Dizzy Bernstein was so named after Dizzy Gillespie, the famous black jazz trumpeter; although Dizzy Bernstein was neither famous nor black, couldn't play the trumpet and didn't even like jazz. I suppose we were a bit short of nicknames for unknown white second-year medical students in those days.)

Anyway, I never gave the matter any further thought (neither did the invigilator) until I came across the writings of a man called Sir Thomas Browne, and realized that the blame for inventing bloody questionnaires is almost certainly his. Sir Thomas (1605–1682) wrote a book in 1646 called *Pseudodoxia Epidemica* which means 'Vulgar Errors'. Basically what he did was to find out what myths and misconceptions were current at the time, disprove them and write down the result. Nowadays he'd be a leader writer on *The Times* but in those days he was just a gentleman.

For instance, he discovered that in the seventeenth century there was a popular belief that the elephant 'hath no joints' in its legs and that 'being unable to lie down, it sleepeth against a Tree', and that all you had to do to kill an elephant was to chop down the tree it was sleeping against, whereupon it was 'able to rise no more'. In retrospect that was a pretty stupid Error for the Vulgar to believe in, but every age has its absurd lapses of common sense – I mean, we've had the Groundnut Scheme, Richard Nixon and Simon Dee. And they've had us, haven't they?

Another misbelief of that time was that if you hung a dead kingfisher by its beak indoors, the dead bird would point its breast 'by an occult and secret propriety' in the direction from which the wind was blowing. Sir Thomas and Lady Browne disproved this by hanging *two* dead kingfishers in their living-room and showing that the birds pointed in different directions. QED. Personally, I'm ever so glad that the Brownes did disprove the kingfisher story, because if they hadn't I think every home in the country would have had a dead bird hanging in the hall for Dad to tap on his way to work; and you would have been able to smell the Meteorological Office from ten miles away.

The point that intrigued me was how Sir Thomas managed to find out what the public was thinking. How, for example, did Browne find out that 'ignorance of the just and proper site of the Pizzel of the Hare, which is aversely seated, ensueth the Necessity for Retrocopulation, and promoteth the conceit that every Hare is both Male and Female'. How could Sir Thomas have found out where people thought the Hare's Pizzel was? After all, it's not the sort of thing you can casually bring into the conversation in a pub. Not if you like your nose the way it is, anyway. Did he prepare a large diagram of the Hare without the Pizzel and present it to the locals like a sort of 'Spot The Ball' competition? Unlikely. Nor can I imagine him saying to some seventeenth-century apprentice fletcher or welkin wringer, 'Dost thou believe that to escape the Hunter, the Beaver bites off its Testickles?' I should imagine that most people would answer that whether it did or didn't could only matter to a female beaver.

There is, I maintain, only one way that Sir Thomas could have gathered all the information he did about popular errors. He must have hired two hundred little boys (which would have set him back a groat and a half) and sent them out with questionnaires and pencils. Like predecessors of the Gallup pollsters these persistent little fellows must have swarmed all over Norwich (Sir Thomas' town), and instead of inquiring: 'Wilt thou be voting for ye Whigs or no?' they'd be asking: 'Dost thou verily believe that the Basilisk can spread the plague simply by the Putrefactive powers of its glance?'

And I suppose that, like most people who are approached by researchers with questionnaires, the Norwich townsfolk said anything that came into their heads. Which is why the absurd belief in the elephant's legs came to be printed; and also why everyone was so surprised by Harold Wilson in 1974.

Well, that concludes my investigation into the origin of the questionnaire. How much of it do you agree with? – (a) all of the above (b) none of the above. You have two hours to answer and don't throw the paper at the invigilator; he's only doing his job.

RESTAURANTS, FOREIGN

As a child I was so sickly and pathetic that I had to be given a complete course of yellow-fever inoculations before I could eat in a Chinese restaurant. However I soon learnt that cultural differences are not necessarily synonymous with health hazards. Having overcome my xenophobia I was once in a restaurant in Bangkok sitting next to an American lady who had ordered steak. She had been unable to eat it all and called the waiter over to ask for a doggy bag. He didn't understand her and she shouted louder and louder, making yapping sounds and indicating a carrier bag in mime. The waiter retired and reappeared with a small bag. When he opened it a tiny dog leapt out and finished off the lady's steak.

When I told the story to a friend of mine he said that if the steak had eaten the dog *that* would have been news (although contravening public hygiene regulations).

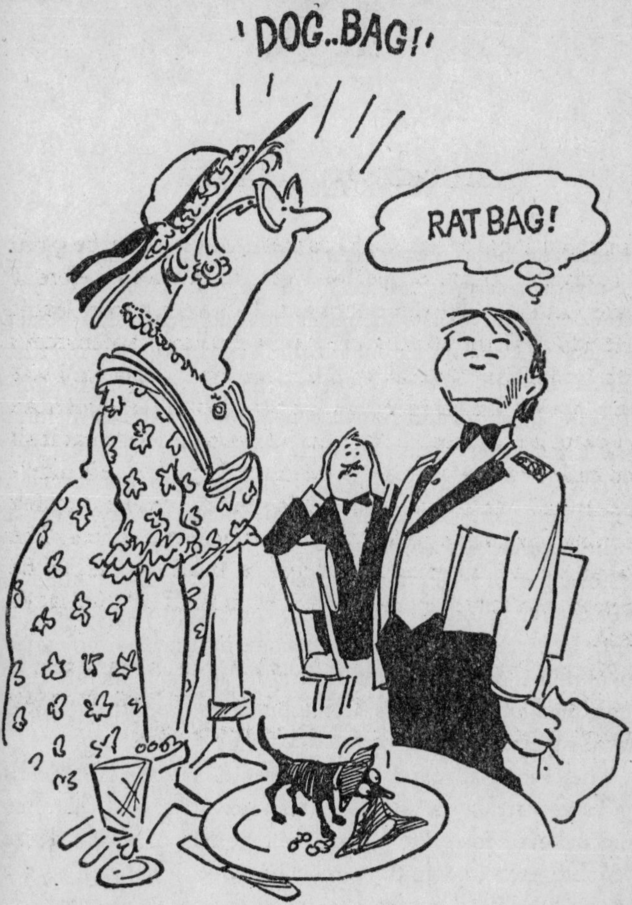
'DOG..BAG!'
RAT BAG!

SEX EDUCATION

Sex education has always been a somewhat haphazard affair. In my own case, it started at the age of seven when my father took me for a walk on Hampstead Heath. He looked at me gravely. 'Son,' he said (I think he'd forgotten my first name). 'Son, the sins of the fathers be visited upon the children to the third and fourth generations.' I stared at him. There was a very long pause. He realized that this piece of knowledge was not having the thunder-clap impact he'd hoped for. 'Son – I mean venereal disease. Always wear a contraceptive. Always.'

For a boy of seven this was weighty stuff; and it made life difficult for me always wearing a contraceptive, let me tell you. It certainly caused some chat in the showers after Swimming. Anyway, what I'm trying to say is merely that sex education has always been a breeding ground for ignorance, superstition and terror.

The Victorians and the nineteenth-century Americans had a very strange set of ideas about sex and sexual anatomy, and believed for quite a time that the seat of sexual desire ('Amativeness') lay in the cerebellum, the 'little brain' at the back of the head, which is actually the organ in charge of organizing balance, muscular coordination and stereo vision. This erroneous belief was elegantly propounded in *The Science of a New Life* (John Cowan MD, 1869). He thought that the main causes of sexual licentiousness ('the curse of our age') were hair buns, tight dresses, boarding-house food and constipation. It's all very logical, because 'the main provocative of amative desires in woman is dress. The constricting of the waist and abdomen by corsets, girdles and waistbands, prevents the return of the venous blood to the heart, and the consequent overloading of the sexual organs and, as a result, the unnatural excitement of the sexual system. In the mode of wearing the hair, the majority of women wear the hair in a large heavy knot on the back part of the head. This great pressure of hair on the small brain produces great heat and an unusual flow of blood to Amativeness and a chronic desire to sexual exercise.'

I interpret this to mean that if you are anxious to prevent a young lady's chronic desire for sexual exercise, you should loosen her clothing and let down her hair. If that doesn't help, consult your family doctor.

And once you've got that little lot sorted out, then you should forbid the use of 'salt, pepper, mustard, salt-food and fine-floured bread, which in their use all tend to constipation and as a result costiveness which irritates the nerves of the *vas deferens* and so is one of the causes of self-abuse in boys and girls'. So *that*'s what's been doing it; I'd often wondered.

But if any man or woman doubts this truth 'let them take a cup of strong coffee or tea and the desire for sexual congress appears at once'. Personally, I always thought it was the after-dinner mints that were causing the bother, and I must admit since I've stopped eating them my desire for sexual congress has decreased most wonderfully and I can often leave the dinner table without congress of any description. My only worry is whether I should tell the Armed Forces of this book, so that they can stop putting bromide in the tea and start putting bran in the soup. Perhaps I won't.

SIGMOIDOSCOPE

A sigmoidoscope is a slim steel tube measuring about twelve inches in length. It is introduced by the doctor into the patient's rectum and has a lighting system arranged so that the doctor can look at the lining of the rectum and examine it for the presence of internal haemorrhoids, any site of bleeding or polyps. Despite the embarrassment and inconvenience to both patient and doctor, the humble sigmoidoscope has probably saved many thousands of lives by enabling early diagnoses to be made. In fact the examination of the lower bowel is so often crucial that there is a famous surgical adage to the effect that 'if you don't put your finger in it, you'll put your foot in it'.

(see *Stethoscope*) (and don't ask why until you have)

STETHOSCOPE

(see *Undressing*) (don't give up now)

SUMMER AILMENTS

During 'flu epidemics, heat waves or rabies scares gentlemen of the press continually ring up doctors (e.g. me) to ask our (or in my case, my) opinion of whatever ailment is all the rage. And rightly so, because we hospital doctors are often the first to detect the seasonal change in mankind's illnesses.

For instance, down at St Nissen's, if we walk on to the ward one morning and suddenly find that it's freezing cold and that the patients are huddled up under their air-cell blankets chipping away at the ice on their porridge, then we

know straight away that it's May 2nd – the start of Official Summer Time when the central heating is turned off. Thus, in our hospital, summer time is associated with an outbreak of acute bronchitis, pneumonia and frost bite of the ears in those patients obstinate enough not to listen to the hospital radio. Conversely, if we suddenly find our necks sticky and our socks full of sweat, we know at once that it's October 2nd – the start of Official Winter which heralds a pandemic of sinusitis, hay fever and heat prostration.

I'm told that in the outside world the seasons aren't organized like that at all and that summer and winter occur at random up to two or three times a week. I can see no excuse for this kind of sloppy behaviour, and I'm very surprised that no one in the Dept. Health & Soc. Sec. has spotted it and sent out a bossy memo to all those concerned.

Anyway, after many years of careful study and analysis I have attempted to subdivide the summer ailments into four groups. Now read on . . .

Firstly, there is a form of low back-pain peculiar to a group of young husbands who have just been compelled to take down the double glazing. There is a similar condition that occurs in winter when they are compelled to put it up again. It may be difficult to distinguish between these two conditions – but although difficult, it is totally unnecessary. Treatment is empirical – that is to say that a doctor involved in the case either has to help with the double glazing or advise divorce.

Secondly, when the pollen count is very high, we often see people turning up in casualty with the nozzle of a plastic nasal spray stuck into one nostril. I'm told that in some parts of Africa this is regarded as a sign of great beauty, but in North London it is usually an indication of great strength (albeit unintentional) and is often the result of trying to use the inhaler on a bumpy bus ride. Some psychologists have interpreted this common accident as a rather bizarre kind of suicide attempt, but in my opinion the psychologists who

believe that do not suffer from hay fever or, if they do, don't ride on buses.

Thirdly, we have frequent outbreaks of a mild viral illness with sore throat and runny nose. We scientists call this the 'summer virus' in order to distinguish it from the 'winter virus', which is what we call it when it occurs in winter. Diagnostic techniques are now improving so rapidly that soon we may be able to distinguish between, say, the July 11th virus and the July 12th virus, merely by asking the patient when the trouble started. But that's just a wild glimpse of the future, so don't go round and pester your doctor for it yet.

Lastly, we have sunburn. Or rather we don't. Now in my five years of medicine I've heard a lot of people talk about sunburn, but I've never seen a patient on a medical or a surgical ward develop it. So my advice to anyone prone to this condition is to get into hospital nice and early – say February – and stay there with the blankets over your head till October. You won't get sunburn, but, on the other hand, the ceiling may fall on your head. It's a cruel world.

Well that seems to be all I know about summer, which is just as well because while I was typing out this bit of the book, I missed it.

SUPPOSITORIES

It continues to astonish me that in these days of digital-calendar watches and lasers very few people realize that suppositories have functions other than easing constipation. In fact in several common and distressing conditions such as acute asthma and migraine, useful drugs can be given in the form of a suppository. The drug is absorbed from the lining of the rectum in a predictable fashion while the patient may be too sick to absorb drugs from the stomach.

However, the confusion about suppositories is not limited to the public. My friend Dave was a casualty officer in the Midlands when a young asthmatic man was admitted with severe breathlessness. Dave instructed a junior nurse to give the patient two suppositories containing aminophylline to help the breathing. After a few minutes the sound of the patient struggling for breath seemed to get worse and my friend Dave rushed into the cubicle to find the former with one suppository jammed firmly up each nostril. 'To help the breathing,' the nurse explained.

Dave said he whipped the suppositories out of the patient's nose and rammed them where they were supposed to be. Apparently the patient was rather affronted, and complained that Dave could at least have wiped them first.

There is another story that concerns a patient whose doctor was very shy, and told him to take the suppositories *per rectum* without explaining further. For some reason the patient thought that *per rectum* meant once every two hours, and swallowed the damned things for a fortnight. When he went back to the surgery the poor chap was feeling distinctly worse and said, 'Those bloody tablets did me no good at all, Doc – in fact for all the use they were, I might just as well have stuffed them up my arse.'

I don't know if that story is true but from my vast experience of the way doctors communicate with patients, I would think it is.

'HERE...WIPE YOUR NOSE!'

TELLING PEOPLE THINGS

Patients are very quick to complain that doctors never tell them things. Often they may be right, and the doctor has been too embarrassed or afraid to tell the patient the nature of the illness or to confess that he doesn't know. However the communication barrier is a two-way affair – or, as they say in TV documentaries, 'a two-edged sword'. (I don't know why nobody has realized that the easy way to deal with a two-edged sword is to hold it by the handle, and keep your head down.) Anyway it is my experience that there are lots of things that doctors tell patients that they don't want to be told. For instance, 'you must give up smoking'.

When we were in medical school, preventive medicine seemed to have a golden future. All we needed to do, it seemed then, was to get out there, point out the dangers of cigarettes, low-residue diet and so on, and in fifteen years they wouldn't be needing doctors at all. There was, however, one snag to this scheme – it didn't work. Nobody wanted to be told things. Now it's not my place in this book to apportion blame: I have no doubt that we, as a profession, are as lousy at giving sensible advice as we are at taking it;* but I would like to illustrate my own progress in this field, and if someone could tell me where I'm going wrong, I'd be very glad if they'd keep their advice to themselves. Sorry, I mean I'd be very glad to consider their advice in the light of future events. There, that's that, so let's get on, shall we?

For a start, I have not met a single hospital patient who

has not had a grandfather who smoked 120 cigarettes a day. This miraculous old bird not only lived to be 97 but even won the geriatric egg-and-spoon race the day before he died. Or maybe it was the day after, I forget. The point is, the minute I drag the conversation round to smoking, I am told about this dogged old man and the way the cigarette smoke must have pickled him from the inside so that he didn't rot like all those namby-pamby non-smokers who peg out at fifty, Doc.

There is no answer to this ploy. Obviously I have not met any of these ninety-seven-year-old Olympic-smokers (of *course* I haven't; they're never ill, are they?), although I did once meet a man who smoked 120 cigarettes a day. He was a TV cameraman and I never once saw his lip without a cigarette hanging off it. When his wife kissed him she extirpated her tonsils. He wanted to know if there was a soluble toothpaste that would enable him to smoke while cleaning his teeth.

Now when I tell a patient not to smoke, approximately 98% of them immediately ask me if I smoke, or if I ever used to smoke. I have tried three kinds of answer to this question, and here are the patients' responses:

If I reply: No, I have never smoked; the patient replies: Well then, you don't know what it's like.

If I reply: Yes, I smoked twenty a day and gave up a year ago (which is true); the patient replies: Well, then, it's the converts that are always the worst.

If I reply: I still smoke occasionally; the patient replies: Well then.

I don't know what to do. For a short time, I borrowed a skeleton from the Anatomy School. What I intended doing was pointing to the skeleton and saying to my patient: this is Mr MacPherson, another four hundred coupons and he would have had the motor-powered lawn mower. (Collapse of stout smoker.) What actually happened was that in the first clinic I tried it out, the patient was too quick for me. He

took one look at the skeleton and said, 'Don't tell me, Doc, he's still waiting for transport home.' (Collapse of doctor's faith in the superiority of the professions.)

I think what I'll do in the future is to invent a grandfather of my own who smoked two cigarettes a day and died at the age of seven. Any other suggestions will be gratefully received and totally ignored. Thank you for letting me tell you all this.

* Since writing this section, this defect in the profession has largely been remedied by the Health Education Council's large-scale, well-organized and effective campaign of advice about positive health, which looks as if it may succeed. I therefore retract everything I've just said.

TUBULES

Each human kidney is made up of millions of little filtering units which in turn consist of a cluster of very fine tubes, called tubules. It has been calculated that if all the tubules in your kidneys were cut open and laid flat on an average tennis court, you'd die.

TV DOCTORS

Medical students of my generation were profoundly influenced by the doctors we saw on television. The first, and I think the greatest, was Jim Kildare. We were suckers for that high drama and that dya-da-dya-DAHDEE-da title sequence. Some of us used to copy it. We would rush down into casualty, push the swing doors open and stop dead,

frozen into some ludicrous dramatic posture. When Jim Kildare did that everyone else would freeze and glance admiringly at him, but when we tried it some Friday-night drunk would take advantage of a figure of authority standing still and put the boot in amidships. I don't remember ever seeing Dr Kildare getting booted in the nuts, but maybe he did and I just missed that particular episode.

That wasn't the only difference between Kildare's world and the real one. Our consultants seemed to be a very different species from the kind and crusty Dr Gillespie. I mean, every week that damned fool Kildare would make some god-awful cock-up or other, and every time, about three minutes from the closing titles, jolly old grey-haired Leonard Gillespie would whip off his glasses and say, 'You know, Jim, the study of medicine is like reading the Bible: the more familiar you are with it, the more you realize the different ways of interpreting it.'

Now I never heard anyone talking remotely like that. For a start it was only very occasionally that consultants spoke to us at all, and if they did they rarely took their glasses off, and never looked kind and crusty. In fact the nearest thing I ever got to a 'you know, Jim' speech was when some Senior Registrar was absolutely infuriated with me and yelled, 'You know, Buckman, you're like a maladjusted truss – you give me a pain in the crutch.' I sent that remark to the writers of the Kildare series suggesting that it would give their programme a more authentic flavour; but they didn't use it.

The next major medical series to influence us children of the sixties was *Ben Casey*. As a doctor, Casey had one readily identifiable asset that set him apart from his predecessors – hair. He had a chest that looked like a lacerated cushion and arms like moss poles. And suddenly everyone in our year was breaking out in epidemic hirsutism. I swear that people were buying their shirts two sizes too small to allow great tufts of hair to stick out through the diamond-shaped holes between buttons. (Incidentally, it used to be said that old-style GPs would listen to their patients' chests through those holes which became known as 'McBurney's Rhomboid Spaces'. Similarly, if a doctor hooked his finger on to the neck of a lady's sweater and pulled it downwards to examine the chest, he then created 'Scruffy's Triangle'.)

Anyway, to get back to the Casey hair craze, a friend of mine called Roger went a step further and actually glued a ring of false hair to the inside of his shirt cuff, so that it would hang over his previously bald wrists. It worked very well, and he had the admiration of the entire Nurses' Home until one day when he had to scrub up in order to stitch a scalp wound. As he rolled up his sleeves, the hair rolled up with them, and a nurse came in and asked him why he had an armband made of hair. Roger tried to bluff his way out, and said that his pet gorilla had just died and that he was in mourning; but it didn't work and his reputation never recovered. Fortunately the Casey fad died out fairly swiftly when we all found better ways of using our hormones.

There was a brief burst of Marcus Welby imitation. This was relatively easy since it only required possession of a motorbike. Unfortunately in my case the imitation was much more difficult since I could only afford a Honda 50, which on the throbbing-virility scale rated just above a hoola-hoop and below a sewing machine. Worse still it had (and still has) an automatic clutch, which I once forgot about when I stopped at a traffic light outside the Nurses' Home. I thought I'd make do with what I'd got and see if the deep-throated roar of those powerful cylinders, or rather that powerful cylinder, would pull in a nurse or two. In fact the engine sounded like a cat breaking wind (yes I *do* know what I'm talking about), and in mid-rev the automatic clutch engaged itself; the bike leapt forward and I found myself spreadeagled across the back of a Morris Minor. I hoped that the sexual symbolism of my motorbike would not be transferred to my present position. I needn't have worried

– the nurses were wonderful and tried very hard not to laugh. So I gave up on Marcus Welby and started trying to be Woody Allen.

Now that my generation has grown up, or rather qualified and become set in its ways, I think influences from television are much weaker (though presumably they are at work on our future doctors, Lord help them). In retrospect, I think our slavish admiration of American stereotypes did very little harm. After all, the kind of self-consciousness that it caused only made us get our hair cut and wash behind our ears; and that must have counted for something. Mustn't it?

UNDRESSING

Most people are slightly embarrassed about undressing in front of the doctor. Even doctors' wives have *some* reservations about it, particularly if the doctor they're undressing in front of doesn't happen to be their husband. And sometimes, even if it does. However to redress the balance (oh dear!), please let me reassure you that us poor medicos are more than somewhat flustered by the sight of unwrapped flesh when we start off.

I don't think I shall ever forget my first experience of listening to a chest. Of all my 'most embarrassing experiences' this was the most most embarrassing. It was in the first week of our Introduction Course when we were so green that we weren't even allowed to wear white coats. After three days of lectures on listening to the heart, we poor 'rookies' were split up into groups of five and marched off to the wards to have a practice. Getting on to a ward for the first time is humiliating enough, but standing there in civvies made us want to crawl through the floorboards. The registrar in charge of us rather relished our confusion (although it couldn't have been *that* long since he'd left it himself) and led us to the bedside of a pleasant fifty-year-old woman.

There must be something in my face that shrieks 'natural victim', because he picked on me to have the first go at this lady's chest. She very willingly undressed and for the first time I stared at hitherto clinically uncharted waters.

'Well, Buckman, get on with it.' I took my stethoscope out

of my sportscoat pocket (yes, as a matter of fact, I *had* forgotten to detach the price tag) and stuck the earpieces in my ears. Very gently I lifted the lady's left breast and put the chestpiece of my stethoscope on her chest. Having done that I suddenly felt very awkward, and had no idea of what to do next. Her breast was slightly flaccid and I felt so silly standing there holding it, as if I was trying to weigh it, that I gently replaced it on the chest over the top of my stethoscope. I found that this rather neatly held the stethoscope on to the chest and, now having nothing to do with my hands, put them back in my pockets.

The sight of me standing there in such an unorthodox and comical pose provoked a great shout of laughter from my dear colleagues. Despite the fact that due to the unexpected sensation of having my ears full of plastic I could hardly hear anything other than the singing of my blood, I nevertheless heard my chums wetting themselves. Somehow I knew I was the object of their derision and turned my head round to try and glare them out. I'd forgotten about my stethoscope, and as I turned my head the chestpiece flew out from under the lady's left breast with a loud sucking sound and plopped into her glass of orange juice.

I don't know if you've ever listened through a stethoscope falling into orange juice, but let me assure you it's *very* noisy. In fact it was so noisy that I let out an involuntary scream and jerked my head further back to try and get away from the sound, which merely tipped the glass of orange juice over the lady's pillowcase.

In that moment I cursed clinical medicine, I cursed the stethoscope, I cursed my ears and their inventor. All of which gives me a chance to tell you a little about my researches into the inventor of the stethoscope and some of the speculations thereupon. Are you sitting comfortably? Then let's begin.

The man credited with the first attempt at listening to the chest through a tube was called René Théophile Hyacinthe

Laennec and was born in Quimper, in Brittany, in 1781. According to a reliable scientific journal (*Reader's Digest*), Laennec thought up the idea when he was out walking one day and saw some young boys sending messages along a log by tapping on it – one boy was tapping while his companion listened at the other end (presumably they were too poor to afford a pair of cocoa tins and a bit of string). Anyway, Laennec saw this and remembered it when he had to listen to the chest of an obese and shy lady; he rolled a sheet of paper into a tube, stuck one end to his ear and *voila!*

Now this is all very well, but at just about the same time another piece of standard medical equipment appeared on the scene – the sigmoidoscope (see *Sigmoidoscope*), an instrument that has saved a good many lives through efficient and early diagnosis.

Yet, despite its prevalence and usefulness, the name of its inventor is shrouded in obscurity – in short, no one knows who thought of it first. But it is this very obscurity that first gave me the clue. The sigmoidoscope was obviously invented at a time and a place when interest in medicine, and particularly in rectal disorders, was growing at a rate rivalled only by that of social modesty and delicacy. Of all nations, it is the French who have always had the most interest in the pelvic organs, and the point of maximum acceleration in the growth of their medical curiosity was in the first two decades of the nineteenth century – to be precise, 1819. In other words, the exact time of Laennec's ascendancy. It is my theory that the modest and delicate Dr Laennec actually invented the sigmoidoscope but was too shy to own up.

You can see the problem. After all, he was the celebrated inventor of the stethoscope – how could he have thought up a similar anecdote about the sigmoidoscope: what could the little boys have been doing to have given him the idea? Let's face it, no doctor whose first names are René Théophile Hyacinthe is going to get away with much when it comes to telling stories about little boys. I often imagine that moment when Laennec sat down with his rolled-up piece of paper and suddenly realized that not only could he listen down it, but he could look down it as well, and even better (eureka!), look *up* it. Then what?

I mean, he was Professor of Medicine at the Collège de France. He could hardly have rushed round there waving a twelve-inch tube shouting, 'Guess what you can do with this?' I think I know what he did. He got a friend to write out a set of instructions and sent the thing anonymously wrapped in brown paper to himself at the college. At the next meeting of the Division of Medicine, he would have produced it: 'Gentlemen, I have just received this strange device through the post – it is either the work of a genius or an unusually graphic poison pen letter.'

Of course, during the 'research and development' stage of the invention, poor Laennec would have been particularly vulnerable. Just think, suppose Mme Laennec brought a few guests home for coffee and caught her husband, the famous doctor, on his knees on the drawing-room carpet with a whole lot of steel and cardboard tubes and drawings of the rectum. What could he have said then? Just making a present for a friend? A surprise for an enemy? An experimental coffee percolator? An anti-tank missile? Yes, he must have been a brave man, that René Théophile Hyacinthe.

Well, that's as far as my researches took me – to be quite frank, I found it all rather arduous. All this talk of sigmoidoscopes gives me a pain in Laennec.

VENEPUNCTURE

Venepuncture is the posh word for taking a blood sample
(see *Jargon*). By tradition most blood samples in the hospital
are taken by the medical students. In theory, this is meant to
benefit student and patient by bringing them closer together.
In practice, it unites them in a bond of mutual terror.

I don't think any doctor ever forgets his first attempts at
bloodtaking. The sensation of sweat and panic combined
with the need to appear cool and self-reliant is, if anything,
the recurrent leitmotiv of a doctor's career, and he meets it
for the first time as he trots on to the ward with his little tray
of needles and syringes and bottles and swabs.

My very first experience met with beginners' luck. Despite
the fact that my hand was shaking like a diviner's rod, I
actually managed to get the correct volume of blood into my
syringe. Unfortunately I forgot to take the needle off the
syringe as I squirted the blood into the sample bottles. This
produces an effect like a soda syphon and I found myself
staring at this frothy mass bubbling over the tops of the
bottles. I had no idea what was going on. 'Erm . . . your
blood seems to be rather frothy today,' I said to the patient,
'are you feeling all right?' My patient (with whom I was
meant to be bringing myself closer) got rather angry. 'All the
other doctors who took my blood took that needle off of the
syringe afterwards,' he said very slowly. For some reason, I
tried to bluff my way out (this is a folly often attempted by
novices). 'Never mind you telling me my job,' I blustered,

'you've got frothy blood. Now you drink less lemonade or else one day you'll be going up in a lift and you'll get the "bends" like the deep-sea divers.' I don't think he believed me.

A couple of days later, I was sent to the Intensive Care Unit to a small American lady. I swabbed her arm, applied the tourniquet and got my syringe all ready. 'Just a little prick with a needle,' I said. 'Sure you are, honey,' she cooed, 'but what are you going to do?' I couldn't think of an answer. I still can't.

In fact, if it wasn't for the patients, most of us would give up in our first fortnight. Some of them are incredibly sympathetic. I remember one war veteran who happened to have a very fat arm. Finding a vein in it was like trying to hit spaghetti in the middle of a pillow. After my third attempt, he very gently suggested that if I held the syringe very still, he would try and run on to it. He told me he'd been at Dunkirk and that I'd made more mess of him than the Germans, although they hadn't been trying as hard. He wasn't the only one to compare my career as a blood taker with Dunkirk either.

VOCATIONS

It is a sad reflection on the declining standard of spoken English that for many years I thought that a Vocational Training Programme for GPs meant they were getting ready to go on holiday and needed practice. I had strange visions of them all attending evening classes in colloquial Bulgarian and having little try-outs under the ultra-violet lamps so that no bronzed foreigner would spot them on the beach as a pallid untrained GP.

In fact, like so many aspects of twentieth-century life, the difference between vocation and vacation is easier to appreciate than define. There is no doubt whatever that Medicine is a vocation whose followers must be prepared to work hard in the selfless service of others, heedless of financial reward and uncorrupted by the power of life and death that they wield. How do I know all this? I read it in a BMA booklet issued to all of us boys in Science Sixth II who did Biology 'A' level.

I shall never forget that booklet. After about thirty pages telling you which 'A' levels you had to get (without telling you how), there was suddenly interpolated a page with a banner headline reading 'Why Do You Want To Be A Doctor?' In case the question was too difficult the BMA presented two lists of reasons for being a doctor and asked us to make our choice. One list consisted of the definition above (work hard/selfless service/heedless finance), which is where I got it from in the first place, and ended with the words: 'GOOD – YOU'RE ON THE RIGHT LINES.' The other list read:

If you want to be a doctor because:

you can make a lot of money at it

there's a doctor in the family and you might as well copy him as do anything else

you like the idea of holding the power of life and death in your hands

THEN THINK AGAIN – YOU'RE PROBABLY ON THE WRONG LINES.

The reason I'd elected to be a doctor didn't appear on either list. The real deciding factor for me was a children's paperback called *The Human Body* by Cyril Bibby. At the age of seven, my friend Richard had a copy of this book, the cover of which bore drawings of naked women and men. He told me that he'd made up his mind to be a doctor and that his mum had bought him the book. With only a very dim idea of sexuality (see *Sex Education*), I nevertheless realized that these pictures were pretty racy compared to the Jane-and-Johnny nature primers we'd seen so far, and I decided there and then to be a doctor. Twenty-two years later, I'm still a doctor and I've still got *The Human Body* by Cyril Bibby, although I've managed to learn most of it by now and, to be honest, I don't spend a great deal of time gawping at the cover. I can get all that at home.

The problem that bothered me at Science Transitus stage (and still does) was the fear that one day someone would say, 'Why did you first decide to be a doctor?' and I'd tell them about Cyril Bibby and they'd say, 'Well think again, Buckman, YOU'RE PROBABLY ON THE WRONG LINES.'

Talking about vocation, one of my friends called John was once short-listed for a job as a Senior House Officer in Neuro-Surgery and then got a better job a week before the interview. He decided to go along to the interview for the hell of it, and when the Professor of Neuro-Surgery asked him why he wanted to specialize in the subject, he said, 'Because the Voices told me to.' Funnily enough he didn't get the job, but even more funnily enough there was no follow-up to the incident. No consultations or home visits were suggested and, for all the committee know, it is quite possible that your local neuro-surgeon is actually a Joan of Arc in a white coat and that nobody has dared to tell him he is on THE WRONG LINES.

Anyway that's the situation as regards vocation and I'm glad to report that most of the people who wish to hold the power of life and death in their hands nowadays work as plumbers. Now that we've reached this point, I realize that I didn't really mean to write about vocation at all; I meant to write about vacations but got side-tracked by my own introduction. Perhaps I'd better keep rather quiet about it and we'll tiptoe on to the next item, which is now going to be in the wrong place but is all about . . .

I've never enjoyed holidays since a traumatic experience at a travel agents when I was eighteen. I tried to book a student train trek to Istanbul during the peak of the Exodus and the travel agent said why do you want to go, and I stammered something about being interested in Byzantine architecture, and he said well think again, YOU'RE PROBABLY ON THE WRONG LINES. No, wait a minute, that doesn't sound right. Let's begin again.

I've never enjoyed holidays. For a start the idea of Getting Away From It All doesn't appeal to me because I'm very fond of my All and far from getting away from It, I spend most of my time thinking how I can take It With Me. The second reason is that I am very frightened of travel agents. As a group they represent a life form inferior to and more dangerous than the sheep tapeworm (*Taenia saginata*) and rank only above estate agents as evolutionary hangovers. They therefore represent something infinitely less attractive than the All as well as representing the only way of getting away from It. So I tend to stay at home and guard my All from the local recidivists who wish to get away With It, rather than From It.

Anyway, I've now worked out a rather neat way of avoiding contact with travel agents. You see despite my rather scruffy and delinquent appearance I have a magnificent telephone voice. So what I do is ring up the agent and say: 'Dr Buckman here – St Nissen's, Nephrology Department – can you get me to Rio de Janeiro pretty quickly?' This gets their interest at once, and they stop being snotty and obstructive and start being servile. I then put my hand half-over the telephone mouthpiece and say 'What's that, Mary? You say the International Nephrology Symposium has changed venue? Oh, I see. (*Now addressing agent*) Hello? Look, could you make that Torremolinos – a fortnight, package deal if you must. Thanks.'

Of course, I have notepaper printed with all my medical degrees to match the magnificence of my telephone voice (actually I had it printed to terrify the Islington Gas Board after they'd broken a frying pan of mine and tried to say it was an Act of God). So the only real problem is if I have to go and collect the tickets personally when my scruffy and delinquent appearance patently fails to match up to my magnificent telephone voice and headed notepaper. I usually get round this by saying that I am Dr Buckman's chauffeur. Or rowing coach. Or delinquent.

However you can't practise the same technique at Passport Control at the airport. That is one place where you really do have to own up to who you are. It's doubly embarrassing for me because my last passport ran out six weeks before my Finals exam and I filled in 'Profession' as 'medical student' because I wasn't too certain of passing and I didn't want to tempt fate. This of course sentenced me to nine years and forty-six weeks of walking around as a doctor with 'medical student' in my passport. It isn't much of a worry now while I look so young and scruffy, but in four years' time I'm going to look a bit older and the air hostesses are going to be wondering why I keep on failing Finals, and shy away from me. As it happens they shy away from me anyway because I look so young and scruffy, so I suppose I won't notice the difference after all.

And after negotiating travel agent and passport control, the doctor arrives Abroad. Now as I see it, Abroad is just a place full of All that should be got away from, the only difference being that it is Foreign All and slightly easier to stay away From. Some doctors do sign in the hotel register as Doctor X (particularly if their name is Doctor Y (q.v.)) in the hope of accruing professional kudos and getting better room service. All that happens is that they get food poisoning fifteen minutes earlier than everyone else and instead of coping with it privately, they have to stagger around as dehydrated wrecks coping with everyone else's. And if that's why *you* want to be a doctor, then think again, YOU'RE PROBABLY ON THE WRONG LINES.

Actually I did have one stab at foreign medicine when I was in Mexico. An American lady of our party had an inflamed ear and I had not appreciated the fact that Mexican Spanish is not pronounced in the same way as the phonetic spelling in my Spanish phrase book. Accordingly when I asked for a bland ointment for inflammation of the external ear, the pharmacist gave me a box of matches. I guess I was ON THE WRONG LINES. Maybe I still am.

WIT

Wit is a fairly common commodity in the medical profession. In fact that's what most people think when they see medical students' end-of-term revues – common. However it is quite possible for fairly average raconteurs to enjoy huge reputations as hospital wits. This is partly due to the fact that in the atmosphere of tension and suspense that hangs around most medical departments, fairly commonplace remarks tend to sound like Wildean pearls and have a very high retail value among the punters.

At St Nissen's I enjoyed quite a reputation as a wit while I was still a medical student, but the reputation was earned by pure chance. In my second year I started to write scripts for a radio series, and used to send in three or four minutes' worth each week. (Actually I've found that the show is still running, but that should occasion us no surprise. I've heard it said that if BBC Radio had been organizing World War II it would have gone on till 1958, whereas if CBS Broadcasting had been running it, it would have been taken off after thirteen weeks.)

Anyway, the week before Christmas I'd sent in a sketch about doctors and nurses. It was a pretty rotten sketch, but it had a line about a patient who had alarm clocks in his socks. The following night I was hanging around in casualty when a very sweet lady tramp was brought in, having been knocked down and slightly bruised by a motorbike. She was a nice old duck and had all her worldly goods carried on her person – two overcoats, three cardigans, a nightdress, two skirts and three pairs of socks. In the Crash Room, we unwrapped her like peeling an onion (that is to say, it made our eyes water) and when we got down to the last sock on her left foot, there was a small travelling alarm clock concealed in it.

I couldn't believe my luck. I'd heard that nature oft imitated art, but I never believed that happened as far south as Euston, and even then my radio script was hardly art (as the letter from the producer said later that week). Just as if it were a dream sequence in a Bunuel movie, the registrar singled me out and said, 'Why do you think she's got a clock in her sock?' And I said, 'Because her feet keep on going to sleep,' and my reputation was made.

It was astonishing how quickly the story got around. Even the Professor of Surgery heard about it and told me the story every time I saw him over the next four years. I even became a casualty officer and a scriptwriter in the hope of the same thing happening again, but it never did and my reputation as a wit and a card rested on that one episode, until five years later.

Now you may have seen hospital doctors strutting around the wards with a red hat-pin in their lapels, and you may have wondered why. It is not a cabbalistic signal to show that they are no longer virgins; the hat-pin is used in the neurological examination of the limbs to see if the nerves that carry the sensation of pinprick are working normally. Similarly, we test the limbs with a tuning fork to establish vibration sense and hot and cold tubes to test temperature sense.

Well, on the strength of the alarm-clock-in-the-sock business and on my ability to polish up the handle of the big front door, I was soon promoted to neurology registrar (after everyone ahead of me had had a go). One of my consultants was a rather bombastic chap who enjoyed discussing patients and quizzing his staff about them at their bedside, and in their hearing. I've always rather resented that style, and it makes me somewhat subversive. There was one particularly nervous lady whose bedclothes he yanked back, pointing rudely at her legs. 'Well, Buckman, tested them?' 'Yes, sir. Normal.' 'Vibration sense?' 'Normal, sir.' 'Temperature sense?' 'Normal, sir.' 'Pinprick?' I handed him my hat-pin. 'There you are, sir, but please don't call me that in front of the patient.' He couldn't think of a reply.

The story got around fairly quickly and I was assured that I needn't think up another witticism until 1983, and that it might be a good idea if I kept off the neurology ward till then, too. I wonder how Oscar Wilde managed. Oh yes, he wasn't a doctor, was he?

WOMB (IMPORTANCE OF)

Many people believe that babies inside their mother's wombs can experience sensations and feel emotions that will influence their lives as adults. This is probably true. In my own case, when I think back to those months before I was born, I realize that it was the warmth, the dark and the silence inside the womb that gave me my deep and lasting love of night-storage heating.

WOUNDS

The following is a recipe given by Paracelsus as a cure for all wounds inflicted by a sword or sharp weapon:

Take of moss growing on the head of a thief who has been hanged and left in the air; of human blood one ounce; of human suet two ounces; of linseed oil and Armenian bole each two drachms – mix well and keep in an oblong narrow urn.

Needless to say, practical difficulties prevented the stuff from being very popular. Apparently those oblong narrow urns were mighty hard to come by.

'I HAVEN'T GOT A MIXER.
WILL A LIQUIDIZER DO?!'

X, DOCTOR

In order to practise medicine in this country you have to be insured by a medical insurance company who guarantee to defend and pay for you should you commit some act of negligence, malpractice or other kind of lethal mayhem. I should add that in order to practise medicine in this country you also have to be a doctor. (If you still want to and you're not, then think again. YOU'RE PROBABLY ON THE WRONG LINES.)

Every year the insurance companies send round to their members a thick booklet setting out the details of some of the juiciest cases they've had to, tried to, or failed to defend. These hair-raising stories are, of course, anonymous and are known in the trade as 'Nightmare Noddies' or 'The Adventures of Doctor X', and they are so terrifying that they produce a very profound (although sometimes short-lived) effect on the reader's medical standards and, occasionally, his plumbing.

Doctor X has thus become the synonym of all that is incompetent, ignorant, licentious and murderous in the medical profession – no mean feat at that. Doctor X operates on the wrong leg, the wrong patient or the wrong frenulum (there's one under the tongue and one under the penis – only one of them is ever known to cause difficulties in sexual activity). He fails to check bloodgroups, names on x-rays or labels on drug bottles. Off-stage Doctor X drinks the wrong quantities of alcohol, and has affairs with the wrong people (i.e. patients) and occasionally the wrong species. In short Doctor X is the embodiment of every patient's nightmare, and I know where he works but I'm not telling.

In fact almost every hospital has a pretender to the title of Doctor X and one hospital I worked at had a very likely contender indeed. He was a very senior physician and had a tendency to regard anything more modern than penicillin as new-fangled. He was particularly poor at interpreting ECGs (see *ECGs*) and would spend many minutes passing the long strips of paper through his fingers, staring at the mysterious squiggles in horror like a stockbroker reading the 1929 Wall Street Crash on ticker tape. However he was a prime bull-shitter and was blessed with a very quick brain when it came to bluffing (or as we call it in clinical medicine 'Water-gating'). My friend Alan worked as a houseman to this Doctor X. (In order to distinguish this Doctor X from any other, I must now reveal that this Doctor X's real name was actually Doctor Y [see *Y, Doctor*]. I hate to betray a medical confidence but at least I've cleared up any confusion.)

Anyway, this Doctor Y (sorry, X) was standing in some clinic or other fiddling with a two-yard strip of ECG tracing when my friend Alan noticed that he (Doctor X) was holding it upside down. Very bravely he pointed this out. Doctor X did not turn a hair. 'My dear boy,' he said, in his best Mr Micawber voice, 'this is such a complicated problem that you have to look at it from *all* angles.'

By Jove, there was some laughing in the pub that night, as all of us downy-chinned housemen retailed the story to our mates. How we sniggered! How we roared! And how we remembered the line for future use. Yes, we all get caught out in some act of monstrous stupidity now and then and I would say that that famous 'all angles' line has saved more reputations than any other since the invention of the 'wife that doesn't understand me'.

When I returned to St Nissen's two years ago I met the second greatest bull-shitter in the world – let's call him

Doctor X². My friend Charlie Fanshawe caught him looking at a brain scan the wrong way round. Doctor X² simply narrowed his eyes and said, 'You have to be *very* good to read them this way round, you know.'

I'm not sure whether that story is really true. Charlie swears holes in pewter pots that it is, but I've seen exactly the same expression on his face when he's explaining to some first-year nurse that his wife doesn't understand him. Mind you I must admit that in Fanshawe's case his wife *doesn't* understand him*, so maybe we'd better leave it at that.

*Nor for that matter do I, but then I'm not married to him.

X-RAYS

There are lots of things that really annoy me when I watch films or television programmes about doctors, but one of the most unrealistic aspects of all is the way every television doctor makes brilliant snap-diagnoses on x-rays. You must have seen it hundreds of times – a very junior doctor is standing quaking on the ward, a nurse says: 'Here's the x-ray you ordered.' He narrows his eyes as he looks at it for about 0.2 of a second and then says: 'We have a 1.2 cm calculus in the middle third of the left ureter – WE'RE GOING IN!' Then we cut to a three-minute scene in the operating theatre and then to the scene where the junior doctor is now President of the whole hospital, or Heavyweight Champion of the World, or some equally desirable position with wealth and fame and a good chance of pulling the dolly birds.

It was never like that when *I* was a houseman. You see, x-rays are really a bit like telegrams in a secret code. For a start, you may not know the code, and even if you do, some idiot in the Post Office may have made a mistake in typing it out. In other words, when you look at an x-ray you have to try and decide whether what you see there (a) should be there at all (b) actually is there at all or (c) is merely a splodge on the film.

Hence when I was a houseman my diagnostic coups used to sound like this: 'Right. Fine . . . this is the . . . um . . . what is it? . . . kidney . . . yes, well it looks normal, doesn't it? Doesn't it? No it doesn't, does it? Does it? Yes it does. Definitely normal. I think. Maybe it is definitely normal. Fine. Now, is there a stone in that ureter? Good Lord, there is! Right . . . WE'RE GOING IN. No . . . it's a splodge on the film . . . isn't it? Yes, it's a splodge . . . WE'RE NOT GOING IN! Mind you, it's got very sharp edges for a splodge . . . could be a stone. Yes it really could be a stone . . . yes, I *think* it's a stone . . . or a sharp-edged splodge on the film. Hmmm . . . well it's certainly one or the other. Fine.' Et cetera, et cetera.

Of course as I got older, I got slightly wiser and better at covering up my quandary. What I did was to observe my senior colleagues and see how they coped when they couldn't make head or tail of an x-ray. Basically, they fell into two broad categories: the 'stamp collectors' and the 'art critics'. The 'stamp collectors' would stare at the film and then, when they realized that they hadn't got a snowball's chance in a frying pan of getting the diagnosis right, they would screw up their eyes and move right up to the x-ray until they almost touched it with their nose; and then try and pontificate from very short range. This had the added advantage that if their pronouncements were wrong they would be so close to the x-ray as to make their speech inaudible anyway.

The 'art critics' tried the opposite approach and backed away as far from the x-ray as possible; this would be accompanied by a cocking of the head to one side, the compulsory narrowing of the eyes and a high-pitched squeaking noise reminiscent of that used by critics when looking at incomprehensible modern art. The 'art critics' sound like

VAN GOGH!
HIERONYMOUS BOSCH!
REMBRANDT!
X-ray
MRS. DORIS GRUNTLEY!

this: 'Oh yes ... the lung fields are (high-pitched squeal) ... mmm ... a *little* bit plethoric, but yet one does get the impression of *very* (squeal, squeal) mild oligaemia in the right upper zone? Doesn't one?' This is the cue for one of the subversive junior staff to suggest that the 'art critic' is talking Jackson Pollocks.

Not everybody of course falls neatly into one of these two categories. Some can't decide which type they are, and thus rock backwards and forwards, to and from the x-ray, with a speed which increases with their perplexity. They're called 'rabbis'.

After my first year as a houseman I tended towards the 'stamp collector', until one day when I was virtually kissing some chest x-rays, a nurse pointed out rather loudly that the back of my collar was very dirty. I immediately became an 'art critic' and carried on in very grand style until an occasion when I was diagnosing some appalling film that looked like a snow storm in Jutland. I was doing my squealing business to which I had recently added the trick of clapping my hands together in rather camp delight ... 'Oh yes (squeal), that left kidney is undoubtedly (clap) enlarged. Oh yes, large left kidney.' And the nurse said that's his chest x-ray. Which is when I decided to become a rabbi, like my grandmother always wanted me to.

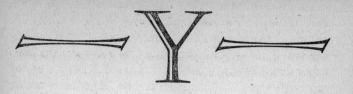

YAWNING

While I was the medical presenter on the television series *Don't Ask Me*, I found that one question puzzled viewers more than any other. The question 'Why is yawning catching?' was sent in by over seven hundred viewers. I avoided answering this question for one reason only – I didn't know the answer; but I'm delighted to say that Aristotle did. In the book attributed to him, *The Masterpiece* (*q.v.*), the problem is dealt with as follows:

Q: Why doth a man yawn when he seeth another doing the same?

A: It proceeds from the imagination. And this is proved by the similitude of the ass, who, by reason of his melancholy, doth retain his superfluity for a long time, and would neither eat nor make water unless he should hear another doing the like.

This may settle the whole issue of yawning, but, for me, raises another fascinating problem. What happens if an ass wants to pass water and there isn't another ass around for him to look at? (*Answers on a postcard to Aristotle.*)

The real name of the man known in the medico-legal text-books as Doctor X (*q.v.*).

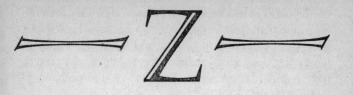

ZYGOMA

If you want to know where your zygoma (or *zygomatic bone*) is, wait until a morning after a night during which you have had little sleep. Now look into a mirror. Are you looking into a mirror now? No of course you're not, you're reading this. Well have you got bags under your eyes? If you have, the bottoms of the bags are resting on the top of the zygomatic bone. The zygoma is a bone shaped a bit like a three-cornered hat, except that it has four corners and bears no resemblance to a hat other than the fact that medical students are always forgetting about it.

The major importance of the zygoma is that it is quite likely to get injured in any situation where the human face (e.g. mine) comes into contact with potentially immovable objects (e.g. windscreen of Beetles' Mini) (see *Accidents*).

Now the study of injuries of the zygoma was first put on the map by a man called Dr Le Fort. Accordingly, fractures of the face are classified into Le Fort Grade I, Grade II etc. I thought that this was a particularly scientific sort of approach and secretly admired Dr Le Fort quite a lot. However I have recently found out that Le Fort did a great deal of his research by dropping bricks on to the faces of corpses, and dropping corpses on their faces on bricks. Of course I know nothing of his intentions at the time and giving him the benefit of the doubt can only praise his observations and industry.

But I do keep on wondering about his early career. How

did he manage at interviews? I mean when they asked him his future plans, did he really 'fess up and say what I'd like to do is bash corpses with bricks. And if he did, would they have said, 'Good idea – someone's got to do it,' or would they have replied, 'Think again, Le Fort – you're probably ON THE WRONG LINES.'

APPENDIX

There is a traditional music-hall joke that runs as follows:

Q: Do you know the way to Borehamwood?
A: Yes, tell 'em about your operation.

It's strange but operations seem to have an *Ancient Mariner* element in them; hardly has the customer come round from the anaesthetic than he's buttonholing the wedding guests and stopping 'one of three' with the story. I'm not saying this in order to sneer at it; I merely record it as a facet of human behaviour. In my case, when I had my own appendix (who else's?) out two months ago, I didn't even wait to recover consciousness (so I'm told), but blathered away like a two-bob watch in the Recovery Suite.

My point in mentioning the whole business is simply that we all take our own health very seriously and we expect our medical advisers to do likewise. This means that doctors – and their patients – are usually under pressure, and I think that medical humour has developed largely in order to relieve that pressure. Humour and medicine are of mutual benefit, and I hope they remain so for ever.

For those of you who were hoping for details of my appendicectomy, all I'm going to tell you is that the surgeon said it was the most inflamed appendix he'd ever seen since last Thursday. Oh, and one other thing – the doctors and the nurses were wonderful.

That is the end of the appendix.

(see Appendix, The)

John Slater
Just Off the Motorway £1.95

The new and enlarged edition of a sensational bestseller.
Introduction by Russell Harty.

Here's the new, bang-up-to-date edition of the handbook everyone
needs. Detailed research, careful sampling, and more than 150 maps
show where you can find any service you require – cheaper and better –
by turning off at a junction and driving no more than three miles off the
motorway – eating, drinking, overnight stops, breakdown services,
petrol, visits.

'Worth a detour to buy it' DAILY MAIL

Ian Skidmore
Lifeboat VC £1

Dick Evans is a man with 'a special sort of courage'. For over half a
century he has been associated with the *Moelfre* lifeboat in Anglesey,
guarding one of the most perilous stretches of British waters and taking
part in some of the most dramatic rescues in recent history.

Evans is the only lifeboatman to hold two RNLI gold medals – that
institution's equivalent to a Victoria Cross. These awards are amply
justified as we learn of his many rescues in storms that gusted up to
125 mph with gargantuan waves reaching heights of forty feet or more.